A Jewdas Haggadah

A Jewdas Haggadah

For diasporist seders

DIVINELY INSPIRED BY
RABBI GEOFFREY COHEN

First published 2019 by Pluto Press
345 Archway Road, London N6 5AA

www.plutobooks.com

British Library Cataloguing in Publication Data
A catalogue record for this book is available from the British Library

ISBN 978 0 7453 3980 1 Paperback

Typeset by Shawn Paikin

Printed in Europe

We dedicate this haggadah to all that sustains us:

To everyone in the Jewdas community, to good quality and plentiful kiddushes, and to the never-ending communal broiges

To our ancestors who fought for freedom and passed down their stories to us, creating and enriching the Judaism that we embody today

To the earth for holding and protecting us, and for inspiring us with its beauty and power

To our descendants who we hope will forgive us for taking time out of making the world a better place in order to laugh at it

A foreword by Rabbi Geoffrey

Afternoon.

Rabbi Geoffrey Cohen here. I'm not happy about it. I've been dragged out of retirement to write a foreword for some piece of banal narishkeit they are calling a 'Jewdas Haggadah'. Unpaid of course, the fucking schnorrers. Don't they know how busy I am? In the time it's taken me to write this I could have ate twelve fishballs and a chollah and cream cheese sandwich. At least.

You see it's all a big fraud. They call me the founder of Jewdas. Feh. I never set out to found anything. I just wanted to get invited to all the posh Jewish parties and move out of my 'studio flat' in Upper Clapton. I thought if I did a few stunts I'd start getting invited to the better kiddishes and get offered a cushy job promoting 'youth engagement' at the UJIA.

Did it work out like that? Did it gehennom. I achieved this weird notoriety and after a while all these kids wanted to get involved, flush with what the goyim call 'ideology'. They actually believe in all this stuff, wanting to bring moshiach 'bimheirah b'yameinu' yada yada yada. It's the classic thing where a great and holy leader creates something and their followers wreck it: just ask Jesus, Moses and Reverent Moon. I wish I could call up my old chaver Rabbi Louis Jacobs. He'd get it, he'd be turning in his grave if he could see what they've done to his beloved scientology.

And what happens now? These kids swan around the world getting interviewed in the press and going to fancy-schmancy conferences, proclaiming a new era of radical Judaism. And where am I, the gantser macher of Gants Hill, the Ilui of Ilford, the Godol Hador of Golders Green? Stuck here in the second to last kosher hotel in Bournemouth drowning my sorrows in Slivovitz.

I suppose at this point I should say something positive. About the benefits of Jewish diversity and how it's wonderful to have another haggadah to add to the field. Sod that. We have far too many already, you can hardly have a seder nowadays, everyone is on a different page. And most of them are too heavy, because they are so filled up with liberal platitudes. Just get to the meal already.

I guess the one good side of this 'Jewdas' movement is that the Jewish establishment hate them. They must be doing something right. Much as the kids drive me nuts it's important to keep in mind that the Board of Deputies and Jewish Leadership Council are total and utter c****.

So that's it. I've said my piece. Just one thing before I go. Pluto Press have said they'll cover any legal costs from the book so it's a good opportunity to settle a few old scores.* 'Chief Rabbi' ███████████† is an intellectual fraud who never actually went to Cambridge, just to an open day. Moses Montefiore was really an Anglican from Devon, he just pretended to be Jew in order to become famous. And ████████████ isn't circumcised. If he disputes this let him prove it in court.

RG Cohen

– Geoffrey
5779

---

* No we have not – Pluto
† Redacted pending legal advice

Dear Bibi,

I am writing to bring to your attention the recent discovery of ancient Jewish scrolls in the Porter Brook in South Yorkshire. Normally such a finding would be widely publicised and celebrated within the Jewish world, however in this instance I suggest we keep this out of the media.

The scrolls have largely disintegrated, but I was able to piece together some fragments and translate the text. The fragments appear to be from a text which has a strong diasporist sentiment, seemingly authored by a 'Rabbi Geoffrey Cohen'.

The text contains instructions for Rabbi Geoffrey's followers to create a diasporist haggadah, which should propagate a multitude of dangerous ideas such as taking down capitalism, instituting global and space communism, liberating the oppressed and dismantling all nation-states.

Following an extensive search of East London, I managed to track down Rabbi Geoffrey's followers, who were singing Yiddish and revolutionary songs loudly and out of tune in a derelict old synagogue. I successfully distracted them with abundant pickles while one of my associates quickly confiscated their papers.

This worrying haggadah has a strong sense of doikayt (hereness) and incites its readers to create radical change in the world.

Worst of all, this heretical haggadah appears to be fully functional, suggesting an intent to enable Jews across the diaspora to hold diasporist seders of their own, which would constitute a grave threat to the status quo and our claim of a homogenous Jewish community.

This is an extremely dangerous haggadah and it is essential it does not get into the wrong hands. I have attached a copy to be analysed by Mossad so we can finally put a stop to this fun, political and joyous form of Jewish practice.

Best, Chief Rabbit Flopkin

Dear Chief Rabbit Flopkin,

Jewdas are a group of self-hating, stupid, childish self-proclaimed 'Jews', who are pariahs among the anglo-Jewish community. They are antisemitic and support terrorism.

I am actually really busy destroying villages and not interested in the internal politics of anglo-Jewry

Please stop sending things to me.

Bibi

– BIBI

A guide to

Jewish Practice in the Late Capitalist Era.

Introduction

Each week at the Diasporist Beis Din of South Yorkshire, we receive countless queries seeking advice on whether porridge made with oat milk is treyf. During Pesach however, enquiries about oats naturally subside, and give way to a wave of requests for advice on how to practice Judaism 'authentically'. Looking back through our records, it is clear that the search for authentic Jewish practice is one that generations of Jews have been struggling with for centuries.

Some schools of thought understand authentic Judaism as a Judaism which resists the pushes and pulls of whatever social or historical context that we find ourselves in. They weave a narrative that our traditions and practices are ancient, that the Judaism of our ancestors was recognisable to the Judaism that we practice today. while some of our traditions are indeed ancient and unchanged from the time of the bible, such as the Havdala nusach,* circumcision and setting up excessive numbers of Jewish communal organisations and then complaining that there isn't one that represents you exactly, many traditions are newer and have been developed by Jews in response to the society they live in at the time.

At the Diasporist Beis Din, we understand 'authentic' Jewish practice to be everchanging, constantly responding to the world around us. For us today, the question is 'What does it mean to be Jewish in the late capitalist era?'. This is not a question which can or should be answered, but a question to be pondered upon, and struggled with. It is a question to write down in a notebook and then lose it, and then find it a few weeks later and be confused. It is a question to be asked in a group discussion, in a philosophical way that will make you look clever. Try asking it out loud now. Try it.

Here at the Diasporist Beis Din, it is a question that we struggle with every day. It provides a framework with which we answer all the questions and dilemmas that our communities bring to us.

---

* While this tune is widely attributed to Debbie Friedman, this does not explain how it came to be accepted and used across all denominations. The only explanation for its ubiquity is that the tune was delivered to Moishe at Mount Sinai.

To be Jewish in the era of late capitalism, is to be Jewish in a time when states impose borders round countries and restrict movement, when we are beginning to feel the devastating effects of climate change, yet governments are still facilitating the extraction and burning of fossil fuels, when the super rich are hoarding the world's resources, evading tax, bombing civilians and generally doing very very bad things.

But it is also being Jewish in a time just before the revolution, where we are amplifying our resistance, where we are winning our fights, where we are throwing parties which are better than ever before. It is being Jewish in a time of fear and of hope, a time of healing and fighting, and a time where ha'olam haba (the world to come) is just round the corner.

We include in this section of the haggadah an abridged guide to Jewish practice in the late capitalist era, inspired by the most frequent questions that we get asked.

Fragments from the Book of Geoffrey

With permission from the European museum of Jewish Diasporist history

This fragment, recovered from the River Don in Sheffield appears to be from the Book of Geoffrey. While some diasporists believe that this was written by Geoffrey herself, from an archaeological perspective, it seems to have been written in 1740, at least 300 years after Geoffrey was born.

Through advanced archaeological research methods, academics at the Diasporist Beis Din of South Yorkshire have managed to reconstruct the text that these fragments came from.

A reconstructed page from the Book of Geoffrey

And you shall hold
A diasporist seder
On the fourth night
You shall lean left
and drink four cups of
wine, and you shall
provide ample pickles
and recount the story
of the Exodus

Rashi: *You shall hold.* You shall host in your home or in any community centre which is affordable to your comrades. *A diasporist seder:* as it will be explained later in the gemara. *On the fourth night:* the halacha is that a seder can be diasporist on any night of pesach but a fourth night seder may not be held on the third night or the fifth night. Why the fourth? The gemara will explain reasons for holding the seder on the fourth night. *The matriarchs:* of the tenach. *Health food:* food for hippies as it is found in Camden.

Rabbi Geoffrey taught: You shall hold a diasporist seder on the fourth night of pesach.

The gemara asks: why fourth? Four is the matriarchs, as it is written; Sarah, Rebecca, Rachel and Leah. But Bilhah and Zilpah is six. Four is the corners of a square matzah. But Rakusens are branching out into the health food market with circular matzahs. Four is the corners of the earth where the diaspora is scattered. But science. Say instead: first night with family, second night with synagogue, third night the community centre was unavailable as it had been booked out by the yoga group.

TOSFOS: A diasporist seder. While much of the Gemera and commentary is dedicated to understanding while the seder is held on the fourth night, the more pressing questions is why we should hold a seder at all given that there is still so much work to do, to overcome injustice.

Rashi: *You shall lean:* to tilt your upper body. But why does it say to lean? This is because it is given that the diasporists are already facing left in all aspects of their daily tasks. *Left.* Why left and not right? Why not lean forward or backward or twirl while drinking? It will be explained that left is the direction of justice and compassion, equality and wilderness. *When you drink wine:* we are instructed to drink wine, not eat it. The leaning must be done at the same time as drinking as this is fun for everyone

Rabbi Geoffrey taught: You shall lean left when you drink the wine at the seder.

The gemara asks: does leaning left only apply to drinking?! Didn't we learn in a Baraita: Rav Audrey taught: It says regarding the tamid offering 'bring it every day [on the left].' And the word [lhakriv] is used there. Similarly the word [lhakriv] is used in regards to binge drinking. The gemara clarifies on Rav Audreys statement: what is meant by binge drinking? Any time that one drinks 'four' cups of wine in one evening. Clearly, leaning left is mentioned in the case of the tamid and therefore applies too to our seder. and can therefore be assumed to be constant.

TOSFOS: But didn't we learn in masechet gittin that one must lean right at all times? However, it appears to us that leaning right is only done when appealing to institutions for funding (example: fundraising dinners when drinking wine must be done in excess) and when writing grant applications. During these times, our practice is to lean right and take selfies with zebras while clapping for Tories. (and qualifying this as a once a year practice).

How to have a diasporist seder

In the Book of Geoffrey 2:14-16 we are commanded to hold diasporist seders during the festival of Pesach – but what is a 'diasporist seder' exactly?

Rashi explains that to fulfil this mitzva, there are two basic requirements:
1. Hold a seder
2. Be in the diaspora

The Jewdas Beis Din adds in one more component of all diasporist seders: diasporist kavanah (intention). A good starting point is to develop a personal philosophy of what 'diasporism' means to *your* community. Diasporism inherently manifests uniquely to each community at each moment in time. But its uniqueness is held by its universality, that is the connection of all struggles and all communities.

Diasporism offers an alternative to Zionism, by placing the diaspora as the focus of our Jewish practice, bringing to our attention the joys and struggles of people both close to us *and* far away. Diasporism invites us to tell the stories of our ancestors' lives in the diaspora, and to dream our own diaspora futures into reality.

To hold a diasporist seder, ask yourself and your community – what are the liberation stories that you want to tell, that you are called to tell? Whose oppression is ongoing? Whose stories are silenced?

Consider what the customs of the seder mean to you. Be thoughtful and joyful with your seder, be flexible and radical.

This is the haggadah that we will use at our diasporist seder in 5779. You are welcome to take it as a whole to use at your seder, however you are also invited to use this haggadah as inspiration, using bits that speak to you and setting aside the parts that don't.

WHERE IS THE DIASPORA?

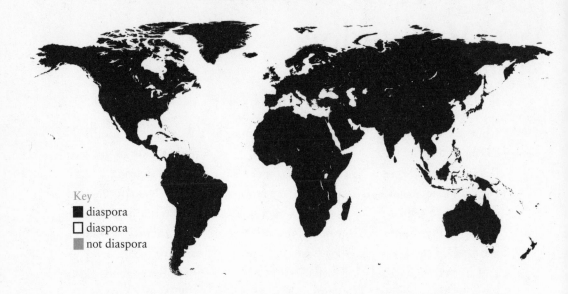

Key
■ diaspora
□ diaspora
▨ not diaspora

GUIDANCE FOR THOSE WHO DON'T LIVE IN THE DIASPORA

If you happen to not be in the diaspora but still wish to hold a diasporist seder, you can observe a tradition started by Rav Freda Bat Levi in Tractate Golus:

ואם נמצאת היא במדינת ישראל בזמן פסח,
תבנה ערוב לחג, והאדמה הנכללת ואנשיה יוגלו

> 'if she happens to be in the State of Israel for Pesach, [then] she
> [should] erect an eruv for the festival [of Pesach], then the land
> and its people [that fall] within the eruv [shall be considered
> to be] in the diaspora for the duration [of Pesach]'

Unfortunately if you live in Sheffield, UK or Sheffield, Massachusetts this exception cannot be applied, but you can still hold a diasporist seder in Rotherham or Barnsley in the UK, or Millerton, NY if you are in the US.

How to hold a seder

Choose a date within the eight days of Pesach. The dates of Pesach move around each year so google it. Traditionally seders are held on the first and second nights, but you can have a seder on any night, or in the morning if you really wanted to.

Invite your community: friends, family, strangers. You can't have a seder on your own, it's a community event. If you don't know anyone, see if you can find a community nearby that shares your values. Hey, new friends!

Worry about food. Either cook or get people to bring a dish. Overcatering is a traditional Jewish value (see *kiddush*, glossary), and we recommend a food-propaganda ratio (FPR) of at least 5. (See FPR, glossary)

Prepare the seder plate (see pages 76–8 for what we are including on ours)

THE SERVICE:

Have a flick through the haggadah in advance and plan which bits you're going to do and which sections you're going to leave out or find alternatives for. Diasporist seders are all unique, created for a specific community.

Find new readings, decide which stories you want to tell. Whose liberation will you celebrate and whose oppression do you need to work harder for?

Though most seders have a 'leader' to keep everyone on track, the haggadah does a good job at bringing everyone to the same level. In small gatherings we generally go round the table, with each person reading a paragraph. In a larger group you could allocate parts in advance and check that people are comfortable reading.

This haggadah has been compiled by many Jewdas organisers, and our varied Jewish practices are reflected in it. We've used a mix of genders for Hebrew blessings, mix of different transliterations and translations.

How to banish toxicity and fear

ANGEL OF DEATH, BLOOD OF LIFE

Passover is so called in English because the Angel of Death 'passed over' the Israelite households during the plague of the firstborn, because of the lamb's blood smeared on their doorposts. This sacrifice is no longer observed.

But this year especially, many of us have felt the cold breath of the Angel of Death, because things are crap, and everything feels terrible all the time. We offer an alternative ritual to protect your home from killing fear and anxiety.

In Mitzrayim we had to kill a lamb for this. If you don't have access to a lamb slaughtering facility, or are vegan, don't worry! All you need is a brush, a Diva cup, possibly a stepladder, and a person who menstruates (ideally but not necessarily you).

The blood of menstruation reminds us of the nourishment of life. Rather than a sacrifice, Adonai desires chesed and nourishing the poor and needy. The observance of this ritual also looks forward to the culmination of the Exodus on Sinai, when we will learn that Adonai is a womb-full god (*el rachum*).

Talmud tells us: when you roast your lamb sacrifice (*korban*) it is important to use a wooden spit, rather than a metal spit, because the *korban* should be cooked only by fire, and a metal spit may become hot enough through conduction that the insides of the lamb are cooked through that (internally) rather than externally by the fire.

Rav Geoffrey tells us: Some people are hilariously viscerally afraid of menstrual blood and this is a great way to get those people out of your life.

This ritual has its basis in the events of Pesach. However, not everyone may be menstruating during the *chag*; therefore it may take place whenever your period falls during the month of Nisan, including if the first day was in Adar.

STEP 1: Acquire a brush. We recommend a silicone pastry brush. Compared with a paintbrush or a makeup brush, a pastry brush traps less fluid in its bristles. It is also better at managing the clumps that can occur in uterine lining, and can be boiled afterwards for re-use.

STEP 2: Acquire menstrual blood. We usually pop a cup in and wait. If you don't know a person who menstruates, consider making better friends.

STEP 3: (the fun one) Standing outside your door, using a stepladder if needed, smear the blood over the lintel.

In your most thundering pillar-of-fire-and-cloud voice,
read out:

And the blood shall be a sign upon the homes where you live. And when I see the blood, I will pass over you, and there will be no plague come upon you to destroy you, when I smite the land of Mitzrayim.

This is extremely woo and you may feel a bit embarrassed doing it and/or wiping it off the next morning. But DON'T! Also if any of your neighbours or flatmates complain, you can call them antisemitic. If any of your friends who don't menstruate complain, you definitely get to boot them out of your lives forever.

Rashi: 'They were given two bloods – the blood of the doorpost and the blood of milah.' To this we add a third – the blood of menstruation.

Then spend the rest of the night drinking wine with friends, happy in the knowledge that you are protected from both the Angel of Death and irritating people.

How to make charoset

INTRODUCTION

After months of research in the Jewdas test kitchen in the heart of West Yorkshire, we are proud to present a magical mystery tour of charosets!

Be prepared for a disturbing resemblance to the Bristol Stool Chart, the only time you will ever need to buy Pesach wine and a very confusing egg.

ITALIAN – Added protein for those looking to bulk up. Takes symbolism to the next level.

12–14 servings

2 apples	Pre-heat oven to 180°
6 dates	Soak raisins in the lemon juice and set aside.
1 egg (hard boiled)	Spread chopped almonds and walnuts in a single layer on a baking sheet and bake until golden brown.
55g almonds, chopped	Grate the boiled egg on the smallest side of a box grater. For the love of Pesach, not the side for which nothing
25g walnuts, chopped	ever emerges and has no conceivable purpose. The one just next to that. Leave (well) covered in the fridge.
25g raisins	Add the dates, raisins and remaining lemon juice to a food
Juice of one lemon	processor and pulse until a ball starts to form. Grate apple on the same side of the box grater as the egg.
1 tbsp fine matzah meal	Combine with the nuts, egg and processed mixture in a large bowl.

Add matzah meal to bind to a desired consistency. Despite our better judgement we must ask that you be conservative and bear in mind that the mixture will firm up after 30 minutes.

Roll into balls and serve chilled. Definitely chilled.

IRANIAN — Would be an excellent centre piece for any self-respecting liberation seder. Plz send photos of sphinxes to @jewdas.

20–24 servings

1 pear
1 apple
100g walnuts, chopped
100g almonds, chopped
100g hazelnuts, chopped
100g pistachios, chopped
175g dates
150g raisins
2 tsp ground ginger
2 tsp ground cinnamon
2 tbsp apple cider
  vinegar
1/2/3/more tbsp sweet
  Passover wine
Pinch of salt

Pre-heat oven to 180°
Soak raisins in the wine and set aside.
Spread chopped almonds, hazelnuts and walnuts in a single layer on a baking sheet and bake until golden brown.
Grate apple and pear.
Combine the roasted nuts, pistachios, salt, grated apple and pear, spices and vinegar in a large bowl.
Add wine to taste; the mixture should be sturdy, coarse and dry.
Transfer to serving plate and shape into a pyramid, cover with cling film and pop in to the fridge for at least 2 hours.

———◆———

TURKISH — Like eating jaffa cake baby food. A gift that just keeps on giving throughout Chol Ha'Moed.

8–10 servings

75g dried apricots
3 apples
Juice of 1 lemon
Pinch of salt
100g chopped
  walnuts

Peel and roughly chop apples.
Combine salt, apples, lemon juice and apricots in a saucepan. Cover with water.
Bring to the boil and simmer until apples are soft (10–15 minutes).
Mash the mixture until it is smooth.
Combine with walnuts.
Serve at room temperature.

YEMENI — A heart stealer and belly warmer. Outstanding ability to cement friendships and matzah.

10–12 servings

175g dates
75g dried figs
3 tbsp sesame seeds
1 tsp ground ginger
½ tsp ground coriander
½ tsp chilli powder
2 tbsp fine matzah meal
75ml sweet Passover wine
Pinch of salt

Soak the dates and figs in the wine. Set aside.
Toast the sesame seeds on low heat until golden brown and fragrant
Add the dates, figs and remaining wine to a food processor and pulse until a ball forms.
In a large bowl, combine all ingredients and mix thoroughly.
Roll into balls and serve.

———◆———

ASHKENAZI — Fails on all categories. Doesn't even bear a resemblance to poo. But points for nostalgia and a homogenisation of all east and central European culture.

8–10 servings

2 apples
100g chopped walnuts
2 tbsp honey
1 tsp cinnamon
¼ tsp ground nutmeg
50ml sweet Passover wine

Toast the walnuts over low heat until golden brown and fragrant.
Finely chop the apples.
In a large bowl, combine the apples, walnuts, honey, and cinnamon in a bowl and mix well.
Add wine.

CALIFORNIAN — Terrified at the idea of a week without avocado toast? Well we have just the thing for you, even if we aren't sure it actually exists.

10–12 servings

1 large ripe avocado	Peel and chop the avocado with caution. Mix with lemon juice and set aside.
Juice of ½ lemon	
50g sliced almonds	Add the almonds, raisins, dates and figs to a food processor and pulse until just combined.
50g raisins	
4 dates	Peel the orange and separate into segments (without the outer skin).
2 figs	
1 orange	Add orange and avocado to food processor and process until chunky.
	Cover with cling film and serve chilled.

———— ◆ ————

ANGLO-SPANISH — This is the real deal. Contains all *Shir HaShirim* ingredients so you know Miriam would be proud.

8–10 servings

2 apples	Toast ground almonds over low heat until golden brown and fragrant.
100g ground almonds	
50g dried figs	Peel and grate apple on the small setting of a box grater. Mix with lemon zest and juice.
50g dates	
3tbsp honey	Add figs and dates to a food processor and pulse until they form a ball.
1 tsp cinnamon	
1/2 tsp nutmeg	In a large bowl, mix salt, spices, apple and lemon juice with the dates and figs to form a thick paste.
Juice and zest of one lemon	
1/2/3/more tbsp sweet Passover wine	Add wine to taste
Pinch of salt	

SHOREDITCH – Impress your friends with this worldly, cultured charoset which shows off your lefty credentials. Best eaten out of jam jars

10 servings

1 Vegan shankbone from your local organic market

200g Dry chickpeas soaked overnight

½ tsp Saffron

0 g Kosher lab-grown bacon

3 mg Za'atar

2 tbsp Edible gold

4 Vellum sheets

12 Gall nuts

100g Existential ennui

Grate the Za'atar and chickpeas. Set aside for 90 mins and add the Edible Gold.

Peel and chop the Existential ennui into Yad sized strips.

Spiralise the vegan shankbone and mix it into the Za'atar and chickpea mix in a large bowl with the saffron, vellum sheets and gall nuts.

Serve at room temperature with a garnish of coriander.

Our Pesach cupboard

How to interpret dreams

Since even before the time of Geoffrey, Jews have been dreaming dreams of overthrowing the mainstream Jewish establishment, abolishing capitalism and instating global space communism.

However sometimes our dreams do not come to us so clearly, and we need the help from dream interpreters to help us find meaning in them. Here we provide a simple guide to identifying and interpreting common themes within dreams.

THEMES:

LADDERS

Ladders in a dream tend to represent one of two concepts. Firstly ladders intruding into your dream can represent the intrusion of hierarchies to our lives, the constant temptation and unrelenting pressure to participate in the capitalist society. Ladders can also be understood as an allegory of the tower of Babel, indicating a desire for global cooperation and mass organising in order to bring about global justice and build tall towers.

STAIRS

Stairs in dreams represent a desire to transcend nationalism and borders. Stairs are often bordered by a wall on one side and a rail on the other, so a person on a staircase has restricted movement, and can find freedom by ascending the staircase to reach their desired floor. Much like a nation-state.

TREES

Trees in dreams generally represent your community. Each leaf on a tree does its part, and together they provide the tree with energy it needs to grow and bring about revolution. No single leaf plays a more important part than the other leaves, and if a leaf decides to break away from the tree, it disintegrates.

DEATH

Death represents the fall of capitalism

CHILDBIRTH

Childbirth represents the rebirth of the Jewish community, a Jewish community which plays a more active role in fighting for justice and liberating the oppressed, and a community with better kiddushes.

The focus on the birth rather than the baby signifies the importance of the process rather than the end goal. The process by which we take down institutions should model the community that we want to create. Authority should be rejected, rather than appealed to. Knowledge should be liberated for all, rather than acquired. Wisdom and truth should be sought in everyone.

BEING CHASED

Being chased is a common theme in dreams and can occur in a variety of dream contexts. Frequently lefty Jews report dreaming of being chased by Jewish establishment figures while holding a Sefer Torah and/or the book of Geoffrey.

This symbolises fear, specifically a fear that the Jewish establishment with its current structure of centralised knowledge, resources and Torah, will keep a hold on their monopoly over Judaism. Alternatively, some dream interpreters understand this as a representation of a desire to practice Judaism without the confines that the Jewish establishment places on us.

How to entertain your guests

While the service of the seder is more than sufficient to entertain your guests and keep them occupied for an evening, you may have moments before or after seder, or indeed on a different evening during Pesach where you are stuck for entertainment. Here are a few of our favourite Pesach past times

PIN THE BLAME ON THE BOSSES

This is a classic party game, and is even better fun if you are entertaining colleagues over Pesach. Simply draw your bosses on large pieces of paper and attach to a wall. One person is blindfolded and spun around in a circle, sufficiently enough to disorientate them. They are then given a list of complaints with some sticky tac attached to the back. They then attempt to pin the list of complaints on to the drawing of the bosses. The next player is blindfolded and given a new set of complaints, and the process is repeated until all players have had their turn. At the end of the game, the winner is the person whose analysis of the power structures at play in their workplace is the least boring.

MUSICAL CHAIRS OF THE COMMUNIST PARTY

Gather enough chairs for all the players minus one. Spread the chairs out in the middle of the room and choose someone to lead the singing of your favourite lefty songs about liberation (or alternatively just create a nice playlist). When the music stops the participants should quickly find a chair to sit on. The participant who is left without a chair must leave the game and a new chair is removed each round.

JINGO BINGO

In this section we also include some entertainment for yourself if you are unfortunate enough to find yourself at a non-diasporist seder. This bingo was created by Jewdas a few years ago and can be used at a variety of Jewish communal events.

JINGO: JEWISH NATIONALIST BINGO

Play this game at any Zionist Federation rally, Board of Deputies meeting or IDF press conference of your choice.

Stamp along. Every time you hear each expression, cross it off the list.

When you finish a row, shout, "Blood on your hands!"

When you get to full house, shout, "War criminals!"

Why not make the game a drinking game? Take a shot every time Palestinians aren't mentioned.

The winner will have an all-expenses paid Birthright trip for much-needed re-education.

STAND WITH ISRAEL	BIAS IN THE BBC	ISRAEL'S RIGHT TO DEFEND ITSELF
PANDERING TO HAMAS	THE WHOLE COMMUNITY SUPPORTS ISRAEL	TERRORIST TUNNELS
USING CHILDREN AS HUMAN SHIELDS	jewdas	WE MUST STOP MIRA BAR HILLEL / JOHN SNOW / AMNESTY / WHOEVER IT IS THIS WEEK
WORRYING ALLIANCE BETWEEN SOCIALISTS AND ISLAMISTS	DELEGITIMI -SATION CAMPAIGNS	YACHAD TRAITORS
ISRAEL'S RECORD ON GAY RIGHTS	CONVERT TO ISLAM	NOT REAL JEWS

How to respond
to media requests

To guide our social media output and response to requests for media, we refer to chapter 5 of the Book of Geoffrey, particularly verses 3, 4 and 12:

> 5:4 And Geoffrey continued: your content should be aesthetically pleasing and contain a strong message. It is forbidden to compromise the message to placate liberals

> 5:12 Audrey, good friend of Geoffrey, declined a request to talk about antisemitism in the Labour Party, as Audrey saw that this was a boring topic

> 5:3 And Geoffrey declared to the assembled: when creating social media content and responding to media requests, the children of Israel should ask: is this a good use of our labour and will this activity contribute to the revolution

We are שומרות "שלישי ליברלי" (observers of liberal Tuesday), and post our more liberal sentiments on Tuesdays. This strategy helps us with kiruv – the bringing in of liberals, and educating them to take more radical stances on the abundance of open letters in our community.

This is a real transcript of an interaction which took place in a private message on our Twitter.

In conjunction with our social media department, and in response to excessive boring and repetive requests to respond to antisemitism, we have developed an antisemitism screening service.

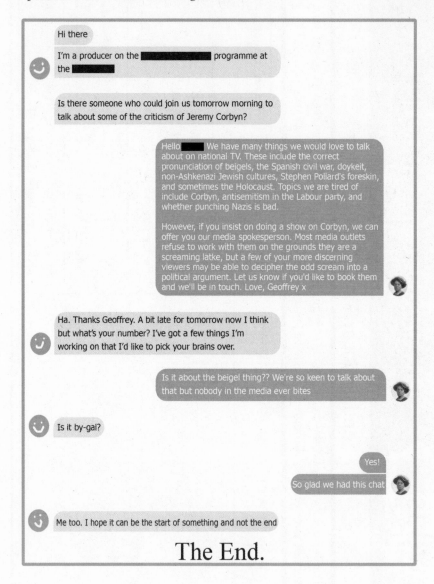

Hi there

I'm a producer on the ████████████ programme at the █████

Is there someone who could join us tomorrow morning to talk about some of the criticism of Jeremy Corbyn?

Hello ████ We have many things we would love to talk about on national TV. These include the correct pronunciation of beigels, the Spanish civil war, doykeit, non-Ashkenazi Jewish cultures, Stephen Pollard's foreskin, and sometimes the Holocaust. Topics we are tired of include Corbyn, antisemitism in the Labour party, and whether punching Nazis is bad.

However, if you insist on doing a show on Corbyn, we can offer you our media spokesperson. Most media outlets refuse to work with them on the grounds they are a screaming latke, but a few of your more discerning viewers may be able to decipher the odd scream into a political argument. Let us know if you'd like to book them and we'll be in touch. Love, Geoffrey x

Ha. Thanks Geoffrey. A bit late for tomorrow now I think but what's your number? I've got a few things I'm working on that I'd like to pick your brains over.

Is it about the beigel thing?? We're so keen to talk about that but nobody in the media ever bites

Is it by-gal?

Yes!

So glad we had this chat

Me too. I hope it can be the start of something and not the end

The End.

Everyone who purchased this haggadah gets a special offer of one free yes/no/ maybe antisemitism screening. Please write your query in the box and then turn to the bottom of page 113 to see whether it is antisemitic.

Jewdas Decentralised Office

Antisemitism Screening Service

Thank you for contacting the Jewdas ASS. Due to high level of demand for antisemitism assessments please submit your enquiry through this form to jewdas@gmail.com Thank you

Please describe the situation, text or image that you would like to be screened for antisemitism:

Please select which antisemitism screening service you would like:

☐ Simple yes/no/maybe answer **£3**
☐ Extended response **£10**
☐ Experienced stylist **£30**

Please pay via paypal to jewdas@gmail.com

Name: .... Date of request: ....

Contact details: ....

All antisemitism screenings will be completed within one week of payment.

The
Haggadah.

MAY OUR SEDER BE JOYOUS AND SOULFUL

May it have moments of loudness and moments of quiet

May it create a space to feel the pain of our own oppression and that of others

And may it create space to celebrate the liberation we have won, and the liberation we will win

May our seder lean on the past and branch out into the future

But may it be rooted in the present

May it be diasporist

May it be revolutionary

And may it not last too long because the food is getting cold and we don't want to delay the revolution any longer

Welcome comrades to our seder

Pesach is naturally the highlight of the year for lefty Jews – the chag of liberation. It is a festival both of celebration and of mourning and struggle. The seder takes us through the story of the oppression and the liberation of our ancestors. We are invited to rejoice in our freedoms, while holding close the stories of those who are not still free and the ways in which we are still not free.

If Pesach is the essence of our Judaism, the seder is serum: diaspora Judaism in 2018, reduced down into one evening of song, brochos, stories and food.

Each year during the seder we tell a story. In fact we tell the same story every year. Year after year after year, we tell the story of the liberation of Jewish slaves from Egypt.

But why? Why has this story been passed down to us, and why are we here tonight retelling it anew? Why should we remember that our ancestors were slaves in Egypt?

Read responsively:

We tell the story of our ancestors' enslavement and deliverance
So that we should be grateful for our liberation and celebrate our freedom

We tell the story to remind ourselves that many people are still oppressed
*So that we should be motivated and inspired to fight harder
for their liberation.*

We tell the story to remind us that we are still not free and
our struggle is not over
*So that we should continue to struggle for our freedom and
bring about a revolution*

If it is the first night, light the candles and recite this blessing:

בָּרוּךְ אַתָּה אַדנָי אֱלֹהֵינוּ מֶלֶךְ הָעוֹלָם
אֲשֶׁר קִדְּשָׁנוּ בְּמִצְוֹתָיו וְצִוָּנוּ לְהַדְלִיק נֵר
(שֶׁל שַׁבָּת וּ) שֶׁל יוֹם טוֹב

Baruch atah Adonai eloheinu melekh ha'olam asher kidshanu ba
mitzvotav vtzivanu l'hadlik ner shel (shabbes v'shel) yontuf

*Blessed are you God, ruler of the universe, who makes us holy
through commandments and who commands us to light the light
of (shabbat and of) the festival.*

If it is the first night of Pesach, it is traditional to recite shehecheyanu, the
prayer we say the first time we do something this year.

We also invite you to recite shehecheyanu if anyone at the seder has not yet
been to a seder this year, or if it is their first ever seder!

בְּרוּכָה אַתְּ יָה אֱלֹהֵינוּ רוּחַ הָעוֹלָם שֶׁהֶחֱיָתְנוּ וְקִיְּמָתְנוּ
וְהִגִּיעָתְנוּ לַזְּמָן הַזֶּה

B'rukha At Ya Eloheynu Ruakh haolam shehekheyatnu v'kiyimatnu
v'higiyatnu lazman hazeh

Blessed are you, God who is spirit, ruler of the universe, who kept us
alive, who sustained us and who enabled us to reach this season

Ale Brider

Ale Brider is a popular song based on the poem 'Akhdes' (*meaning Unity*) by socialist Jewish poet Morris Winchevsky in 1890. The poem is satirical, highlighting the problems that the Bundists had with the concept of Jewish unity. The imposition of 'unity' by the Jewish establishment at the time did more than just overlook the clear disunity among Jews, but erased the oppression of the working classes and the existence of political differences. This song resonates with our diasporist Jewish communities today who are often asked to suppress our political differences for the sake of presenting an image of a united Jewish community.

EXTRACT FROM AKHDES:

Kurtse peyes, lange peyes
Yidn mit un on matbeyes
Frume kep un kep fun zinders
Kep in yarmelkes, tsilinders
Ale zaynen nor eyn folk

Short sidelocks, long sidelocks
Jews with and without money
Religious heads and heads of sinners
Heads in skullcaps, top hats
But everyone is one people

From the incredible research by historian and Yiddish singer Vivi Lachs, as contained in her book *Whitechapel Noise: Jewish Immigrant Life in Yiddish Song and Verse, London 1884–1914*, Wayne State University Press, 2018.

Un mir zaynen ale brider,	And we are all brothers,
oy, oy, ale brider,	Oy, oy, all brothers,
un mir zingen sheyne lider,	And we sing nice songs,
oy, oy, oy!	Oy, oy, oy.
Un mir haltn zikh in eynem,	And we stick together,
oy, oy, zikh in eynem,	Oy, oy, stick together,
azelkhes iz nishto bay keynem,	As nobody else does,
oy, oy, oy.	Oy, oy, oy.
Un mir zaynen ale shvester,	And we are all sisters,
oy, oy, ale shvester,	Oy, oy, all sisters,
Azoy vi Rokhl, Rus un Ester,	As are Rachel, Ruth and Esther,
oy, oy, oy!	Oy, oy, oy.
Un mir zaynen ale eynik,	And we are all united,
oy, oy, ale eynik,	Oy, oy, all united,
Tsi mir zaynen fil tsi veynik,	Whether we are many or few,
oy, oy, oy!	Oy, oy, oy.
Un mir libn zikh dokh ale,	And we love each other,
Oy, oy, zikh dokh ale,	Oy, oy, each other,
Vi a kale mit a kale,	Like a bride with a bride,
oy, oy, oy!	Oy, oy, oy.
Un mir zaynen ale freylekh,	And we are all happy,
Oy, oy, ale freylekh,	Oy, oy, are happy,
Vi Yonasen un Dovid haMeylekh	Like Jonathan and Kind David
Oy, oy, oy!	Oy, oy, oy!
Un mir zaynen freylekh munter,	And we are happy and cheerful,
Oy, oy, freylekh munter,	Oy, oy, happy and cheerful,
Zingen lider, tantsn unter,	We sing and we hop around,
oy, oy, oy.	Oy, oy, oy.

לאָמיר גריבער

און מיר בײַנען אַלע גריבער
אוי, אוי, אַלע גריבער
און מיר בײַנען שײַנע ליבצה
אוי, אוי, אוי!

און מיר האָבן זיך אין איינעם
אוי, אוי, זיך אין איינעם
אַרבעטן אַז נעמען גײַ קיינעס
אוי, אוי, אוי!

און מיר בײַנען אַלע אוסטער
אוי, אוי, אַלע אוסטער
אַזוי ווי רחל, רות און אסתר
אוי, אוי, אוי!

און מיר בײַנען אַלע אײניק
אוי, אוי, אַלע אײניק
3 מיר בײַנען פֿון 3 ווײניק
אוי, אוי, אוי!

און מיר ליבן זיך באַלד אַלע
אוי, אוי, זיך באַלד אַלע
ווי אַ כלה מיט אַ כלה
אוי, אוי, אוי!

און מיר בײַנען אַלע פֿרײַלעך
אוי, אוי, אַלע פֿרײַלעך
ווי יהונתן און דוד המלך
אוי, אוי, אוי!

און מיר בײַנען פֿרײַלעך מונטער
אוי, אוי, פֿרײַלעך מונטער
קיין ליבצה אַזוי אונטער
אוי, אוי, אוי!

Seder of the Seder

We embrace changing traditions and making them new. But even the most committed anarchist and radical Jews hold some Jewish traditions sacrosanct. One such tradition is the order of the seder.

As Bellegarrigue said, 'anarchy is order' and therefore we can infer that order is anarchy.

There are not many absolute red lines in our understanding of diasporism, however doing the seder in the right order is a red line. Going out of order should be considered in the same way as crossing a picket line (which happens to be one of our very few red lines) or building settlements beyond the green line.

Blessing over Wine	קדש	Kadesh
Handwashing	ורחץ	Urchatz
Eating a green vegetable	כרפס	Karpas
Breaking the middle motze	יחץ	Yachatz
Telling the Exodus story	מגיד	Maggid
Handwashing	רחצה	Rachtzah
Eating the motze	מוציא מצה	Motzi, Motze
Eating the bitter herb	מרור	Maror
Eating the Hillel sandwich	כורך	Koreich
Eating the meal	שלחן עורך	Shulchan oreich
Eating the afikomen	צפון	Tzafun
Gratitude	ברך	Bareich
Songs of praise	הלל	Hallel
Conclusion	נרצה	Nirtzah

First cup
Kadeish קדש

A BLESSING FOR THE EARTH!

One of the major tenets of radical Judaism is Tikkun Olam - healing the world. This year, we've learned that we literally have eleven years to fix everything [instruction to reader: insert latest facts about global warming, who knows how bad it's gonna be by April.] We've massively fucked this up, even more than we thought we had this time last year, and the world is dying. We as humans cannot withstand the great forces of destruction that the earth is capable of, be it hurricanes or heatwaves, floods or wild fires, our only hope is to stop the destruction of the earth's cycles and work urgently to heal it, so we can again be cradled by the earth rather than kicked by it.

As we drink this first cup, we pray for the life sustaining earth and commit to do our own part to liberate her natural rhythms from the oppression of human, capitalist exploitation. We also say a hearty Shekoyokh to climate activists like the UK's Fracking Four, who recently won a massive victory.

Rav Trashi adds that if you are doing this in plastic cups, you are doing it wrong. But as Rav Geoffrey teaches, there is no ethical consumption under capitalism other than buying this Haggadah.

בְּרוּכָה אַתְּ יָהּ אֱלֹהֵינוּ רוּחַ הָעוֹלָם בּוֹרֵאת פְּרִי הַגָּפֶן

Brucha at yah, eloheinu Ruach ha'olam, boreit pri hagafen

Blessed are you eternal God, creator of the earth who brings fruit from the vine

Hand washing
Urchatz ורחץ

The first handwashing takes place in silence. In this silence we reflect on the loss we suffer when people, especially those whose identities and politics challenge social norms, are silenced.

Karpas כרפס

As we take the karpas (a fresh green herb) we are reminded of spring: a time when the summer's warmth overcomes the winter's frost, when the wilderness overflows with new life in green leaves and baby animals (in particular we think about baby hedgehogs), and when the bud of revolution blossoms.

We dip the karpas in salt water and recite

בָּרוּךְ אַתָּה ה', אֱלֹהֵינוּ מֶלֶךְ הָעוֹלָם,
בּוֹרֵא פְּרִי הָאֲדָמָה.

Barukh atah Adonai eloheinu melekh ha'olam borey porey ha'adamah

Blessed are you, Lord our God, King of the universe, who creates the fruit of the earth

THE INTERNATONALE דער אינטערנאַצִיאָנאַל

After we have eaten the Karpas, we sing the Internationale, a song which, like the karpas, reminds us of the blossoming bud of revolution.

Original lyrics by Eugene Pottier, Paris 1871
Set to music by Pierre De Geyter 1888

Arise ye workers from your slumbers
Arise ye prisoners of want
For reason in revolt now thunders
And at last ends the age of can't
Away with all your superstitions
Servile masses arise, arise
We'll change henceforth the old tradition
And spurn the dust to win the prize

So comrades, come rally
And the last fight let us face
The Internationale unites the human race

No more deluded by reaction
On tyrants only we'll make war
The soldiers too will take strike action
They'll break ranks and fight no more
And if those cannibals keep trying
To sacrifice us to their pride
They soon shall hear the bullets flying
We'll shoot the generals on our own side

No saviour from on high delivers
No faith have we in prince or peer
Our own right hand the chains must shiver
Chains of hatred, greed and fear
E'er the thieves will out with their booty
And give to all a happier lot
Each at the forge must do their duty
And we'll strike while the iron is hot

שטייט אויף, איר אַלע, ווער ווי שקלאַפֿן,
אין הונגער לעבן מוז, אין נויט!
דער גייסט - ער קאָכט, ער רופֿט צו וואָפֿן
אין שלאַכט אונדז פֿירן איז ער גרייט.
די וועלט פֿון גוואַלדטאַטן און ליידן
צעשטערן וועלן מיר און דאַן
פֿון פֿרייַהייט, גלייַכהייט אַ גן־עדן
באַשאַפֿן וועט דער אַרבעטסמאַן

דאָס וועט זײַן שוין דער לעצטער
און ענטשידענער שטרײַט!
מיט דעם אינטערנאַציאָנאַל
שטייט אויף, איר אַרבעטסלײַט!

נײן, קיינער וועט אונדז ניט באַפֿרײַען:
ניט גאָט אַליין און ניט קיין העלד-
מיט אונדזער אייגענעם כּלי־זײן
דערלייזונג ברענגען מיר דער וועלט.
אַראָפ דעם יאָך! גענוג געליטן,
גענוג פֿאַרגאָסן בלוט און שווייס!
צעבלאָזט דעם פֿײַער, לאָמיר שמידן
כּל־זמאַן דאָס אײַזן איז נאָך הייס!

דער אַרבעטסמאַן וועט זײַן מעמשלה
פֿערשפּרייטן אויף דער גאַנצער ערד,
און פֿאַראַזיטן די מפּלה
באַקומען וועלן פֿון זײַן שווערד
די גרויסע שטורעם־טעג זיי וועלן
נאָר פֿאַר טיראַנען שרעקלעך זײַן;
זיי קאַנען אָבער ניט פֿאַרשטעלן
פֿון אונדז די העלע זונען־שײַן

Shtayt oyf ir ale, ver vi shklafn
in hinger leybn miz, in noit
der gayst - er kokht, er rift tsi wafn
in shlakht indz firn iz er greyt.
di velt fin gwaldtatn in laydn
tseshtern weln mir in dan:
fin frayheyt, glaykhheyt a Gan-Aydn
bashafn vet der arbetsman.

Dus vet zayn shoyn der letster
in antshaydener shtrayt
mit dem internatsyonal
shtayt oyf, ir arbetsleyt.

Nayn, kayner vet indz nisht bafrayen,
nisht Got alayn in nisht kayn held,
mit indzer eygenem kley-zayin
derleyzung brengen mir der velt.
arup dem yokh! genig gelitn!
genig fargosn blit in shvays!
tsebluzt dus fayer, lomir shmidn
kol-zman dus ayzn iz nokh hays!

Der arbetsman vet zayn memshule
farshpraytn oyf der gantser erd
in parazitn di mapule
bakimen veln fin zayn shverd.
di groyse shturemteg zay veln
nor far tiranen shreklekh zayn
zay konen ober nisht farshteln
far indz di hele zinen-shayn

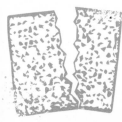

Yachatz יחץ

BREAKING OF THE AFIKOMEN

Take the middle motze and break it in half. The larger of the two pieces is the afikomen and is hidden at this point in the seder.

The smaller half and the remaining two motzes are held up:

הָא לַחְמָא עַנְיָא דִּי אֲכָלוּ אַבְהָתָנָא בְּאַרְעָא דְמִצְרָיִם.
כָּל דִּכְפִין יֵיתֵי וְיֵיכֹל, כָּל דִּצְרִיךְ יֵיתֵי וְיִפְסַח.
הָשַׁתָּא הָכָא, לְשָׁנָה הַבָּאָה בְּאַרְעָא דְיִשְׂרָאֵל.
הָשַׁתָּא עַבְדֵי, לְשָׁנָה הַבָּאָה בְּנֵי חוֹרִין.

Ha lachma anya di achalu avhatana b'ara d'mitzrayim. Kol dichfin yeitei v'yeichol, kol ditzrich yeitei v'yifsach. Hashata hacha, l'shanah habaah b'ara d'Yisrael. Hashata avdei, l'shanah habaah b'nei chorin

This is the bread of affliction that our ancestors ate in the land of Egypt.
Anyone who is hungry should come and eat
Anyone who is in need should come and join our seder.
Now we are here, next year we will be in the land of Israel;
This year we are slaves, next year we will be free people

TOP TIPS FOR HIDING AFIKOMEN

After years of doing seders in the same house, it can be difficult to find novel hiding places and so the afikomen tends to get hidden in one of three places: within the pages of Red Rosa on the bottom shelf in the front room, behind the framed portrait of Emma Goldman in the hallway or wrapped in the 'Mir Veln Zey Iberlebn' banner in the cupboard under the stairs.

IN TRACTATE PESACH:

Rabbi Carys of Cwm Penmachno asked: we are instructed to hide the afikomen in a different place each year, but surely we will eventually run out of hiding places?

Rabbi Audrey replied: One must imagine that they are a multinational company seeking hiding places in off-shore tax havens for their profits. The hider of the afikomen must place the afikomen in the place in their home which most resembles the Cayman Islands.

a prayer for the diaspora

ELPHABA MOND

Shekhinah
Great Mystery
Universe and That which holds you in place,

we thank you for this abundant planet - your own palm of
blessing;
we thank you for this world, our home, that is given with such
love and devotion.

we stand in the open fields of diaspora and know we are blessed

diaspora from the time before we can remember,
  from the pool of the womb,
      from the lands we were forced from
          and the lands we choose

    where we have come from has blurred,
  but our roots emerge like wings
      wherever we find ourselves

            and we are learning along the way
            that where we come from and where we
            are cannot be separated,
          they dance together like the dust of
              the earth
                  from which we came.

  We trust in these winged roots

  we trust in this dust.

our family scattered like holy rain, river-veins kissing
the skins of the spinning earth,
we are like these flowing rivers of not knowing
but all the same,
      leaping, like the salmon towards the source

and the source is you Great Mystery, goddess of courage,
of journeying and justice, of apples plucked from the
sacred Sheffield tree.

We cannot go back to the womb so we sit under this
tree where we find ourselves
remembering our journey is through time and not space.
and Time will never make an exile of us.
And so we live, flames in holy time

Great Mystery may you bless this family, all of us, finding our
way through this earth-dream,
dear goddess,
please, hold us in your tiny palm of our great green and
                                    tiny planet

Let us make holy home on the road,
                                    under the tree,
            in deep family with our neighbours,
                                    of all creed,
                                              creature
                                    and species
                    safe, celebrated, befriended

    and may our diaspora, cold, mossy, green
rainfilled   be our peace
            may we seak peace
            may we know peace
            may we be the keepers of peace

    wrap us in your diaspora,
                oh Mystery,
            So we may be home
            wherever we land
                    keep us safe in your Time
                        remember us.

Maggid מגיד

INTRODUCTION

We're here, at the maggid, or the story telling. This is the highlight of the seder: the charoset of a hillel sandwich. Not only because it has major potential for radical, topical rewrites, but also because the story was made for lefty diasporas.

Standing up to oppression, the failure of liberal diplomacy, collectivisation, increasingly radical direct action, awkward leadership, fun waterside drumming and a long march. Tick tick tick!

Yet if your early Jewish education was anything like ours, the story of Exodus was disappointingly literalised. Look what the goyim always do to us? As soon as you get a whiff of antisemitism, get the fuck out, and by the way your final destination should be Israel. Hmm, bit revisionist?

Tonight, even more than on all other nights, we revel and delight in collective liberation. In staying put exactly where we are until the struggle is over (apart from going on Birthwrong). In coming together with other oppressed peoples with strong hands and outstretched arms. In overthrowing capitalism. In liberating all of us. In escalating direct actions and vigorously debating the use of violence and/or menstrual blood. In our unity with all humanity and life on earth. In our capacity for peace, justice and freeing ourselves. And in our capacity to go more than a week without beigels.

4 AND 20 QUESTIONS

We kick off the maggid by asking some questions

Judaism loves the number four. So in addition to the traditional 4 questions, we've given you four more sets of Four Questions, for whatever Passover situation you may find yourselves in.

מַה נִּשְׁתַּנָּה הַלַּיְלָה הַזֶּה מִכָּל הַלֵּילוֹת?

What differentiates this night from all nights?

שֶׁבְּכָל הַלֵּילוֹת אָנוּ אוֹכְלִין חָמֵץ וּמַצָּה, הַלַּיְלָה הַזֶּה – כֻּלּוֹ מַצָּה.

On all nights we eat chameitz and matzah; this night, only matsa?

שֶׁבְּכָל הַלֵּילוֹת אָנוּ אוֹכְלִין שְׁאָר יְרָקוֹת – הַלַּיְלָה הַזֶּה (כֻּלּוֹ) מָרוֹר.

On all nights we eat other vegetables; tonight (only) maror.

שֶׁבְּכָל הַלֵּילוֹת אֵין אָנוּ מַטְבִּילִין אֲפִילוּ פַּעַם אֶחָת – הַלַּיְלָה הַזֶּה

On all nights, we don't dip, even one time; tonight twice.

שְׁתֵּי פְעָמִים. שֶׁבְּכָל הַלֵּילוֹת אָנוּ אוֹכְלִין בֵּין יוֹשְׁבִין וּבֵין מְסֻבִּין – הַלַּיְלָה הַזֶּה כֻּלָּנוּ מְסֻבִּין

On other nights, we eat either sitting or reclining; tonight we all recline

VARIATIONS ON THE TRADITIONAL

1. On all other nights we eat chameitz and matzah. Tonight, have we bought enough laxatives to deal with the fall out of our matzah-based diet?
2. On all other nights we eat all vegetables. Tonight, are we going to take a tiny sliver of maror hidden between two giant wedges of matzah, or are we going to make our ancestors proud by chewing through a piece of maror the size of our head?
3. On all other nights, we do not dip our food even once. Tonight, why not dip it low, bring it up slow, roll it all around, poke it out, let our back go?
4. On all other nights, we eat either upright or reclining. Tonight, what shall we do with our freedom to cast off the demands of being upright members of our community?

FOUR FOR GOYIM

1. On all other nights, you bring up the State of Israel as a litmus test to determine whether Jews are the 'correct' type of Jews for you. Tonight, why not try something different, and not do that you weirdos?
2. On all other nights, you misreport on the basic customs and facts of our religion. Tonight, why not read a Wikipedia page before writing a headline news article about us?
3. On all other nights, you pick and choose what reports of antisemitism to take seriously based on whether the accused person comes from your political faction. Tonight, why not commit to fighting all antisemitism, even when it's your comrades in the wrong?
4. On all other nights, you stereotype Jews as uniformly white, Ashkenazi and wealthy. Tonight, why not learn more about the true diversity of our community?

FOUR FOR YOUR LOCAL SYNAGOGUE

1. At other times, you serve terrible wine at kiddish. When can we get something decent in?
2. At other times, you put out awfully wishy-washy statements on the State of Israel. When will you condemn Israel's actions without talking about violence 'on both sides'?
3. At other times, you allow Rabbis to play bongos during prayer services. When will you put a stop to this?
4. At other times, you allow nationalist and chauvinist ideas of Judaism to put a wedge between us and our neighbours of different faiths. When will you recognise that joining forces with our oppressed siblings is the only way to secure a lasting and peaceful Jewish future in the diaspora?

FOUR FROM THE BUND HAGGADAH

1. Ma nishtana, how are we worse off than Shmuel the manufacturer, from Meir the banker, from Zarah the moneylender, from Reb Turdus the Rabbi? They do nothing and have food and drink, both by day and night a hundred times over, and we toil with all our strength the entire day, and at night we don't even have a meal, as well?
2. They have great castles, shown off and drubbed up with all the trappings, beautiful rooms standing unbelievably empty – and we lie stuck together in a hole and they even want to throw us out of there?
3. They do nothing and wear the most expensive clothes – and we toil like oxen and have not a shirt on our bodies?
4. They eat a hearty dinner, drink a full-bodied glass of wine and go to sleep in a spacious warm bed and 'Everything goes well among us' and we lay ourselves down in a tiny corner on a straw mattress so that we can soon awaken to work?

These four questions are taken from the haggadah published by the United Jewish Labour Bund in Russia and Poland in 1900. The translation from Yiddish is by Fern Kant, Workmen's circle, Philadelphia, as found in 'Of Moses and Marx: Folk Ideology and Folk History in the Jewish Labor Movement' by David Philip Shuldiner

4 The four comrades

The wise comrade asks:

'but what does karl marx actually say we should do?
How do we bring about communism?'

This is a good comrade. You should immediately assign them all your union's organisational and admin tasks.

The wicked comrade asks:

'what are you even doing? This is pointless, what about human nature, history has proven communism doesn't work, jeremy corbyn is unelectable. What would the revolution do for me?'

Notice how they say for 'me' and not for us. This douchebag is not your comrade. According to the rabbis and chabad.org, you should 'blunt their teeth'.

The simple comrade asks:

'if what you are doing is good, why do you cover your faces in front of the police?'

This comrade is still a comrade and you should be patient with them. You should remind them all cops are bastards and point them to reporting about undercover cops, falsified evidence and abuse of power. Then sing daloy politsey at them until they join in.

The comrade who does not know how to ask

This is probably because some overconfident white men (and probably a few privately educated white women) are dominating the whole conversation. You should tell the people who are taking up too much space that they are taking up too much space, and buy some more wine. Wine relaxes people and then the comrades who haven't spoken yet might. Also ask them if they want to speak.

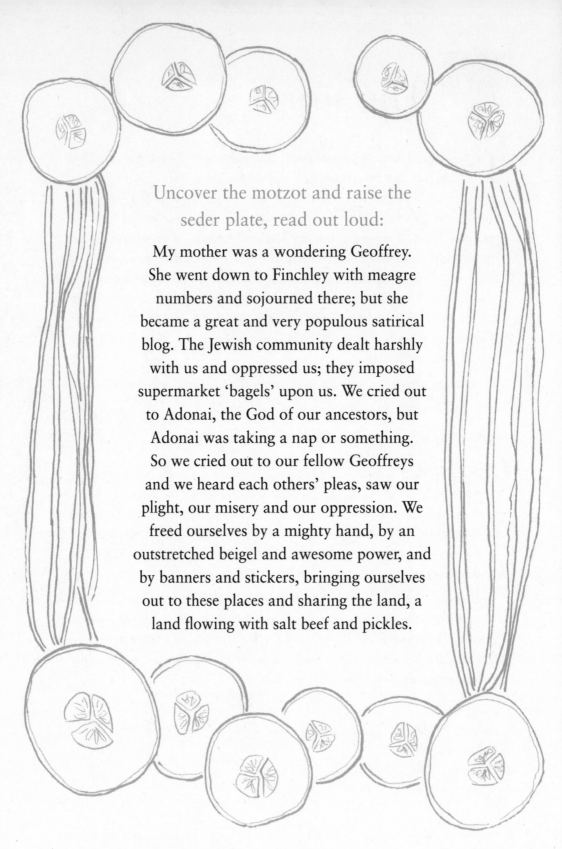

My mother was a wondering Geoffrey.
She went down to Finchley with meagre
numbers and sojourned there; but she
became a great and very populous satirical
blog. The Jewish community dealt harshly
with us and oppressed us; they imposed
supermarket 'bagels' upon us. We cried out
to Adonai, the God of our ancestors, but
Adonai was taking a nap or something.
So we cried out to our fellow Geoffreys
and we heard each others' pleas, saw our
plight, our misery and our oppression. We
freed ourselves by a mighty hand, by an
outstretched beigel and awesome power, and
by banners and stickers, bringing ourselves
out to these places and sharing the land, a
land flowing with salt beef and pickles.

The story

In the haggadah we are instructed to tell the story of the Exodus as if we ourselves had been there in Egypt. Most seders focus on the famous parts of the Exodus story: the working conditions imposed upon the Israelites by Pharaoh, the ten plagues and the escape across the Red Sea into the desert. They leave out the less well-known parts, such as when the Israelites successfully nationalised healthcare in Ancient Egypt, ensuring that healthcare was publically funded, publically provided and free at the point of use. The midrash of how the Ancient Israelites came together with working class Egyptians to organise direct action to stop the government dumping toxic waste into the Nile is also ignored by most mainstream Jewish communities.

In this re-enactment, we tell the midrash of the Israelites campaigns around land rights.

SCENE 1:

NARRATOR: It is hard to imagine life in Ancient Egypt, but we will do our best to set the scene. For several decades before the birth of Moses, the divide between the rich and the poor had been getting bigger. The Ancient Israelites worked long hours (or sometimes very short hours, as they were on zero-hour contracts), building swanky pyramids and fancy dwellings.

However they were paid so little that they could never dream of being able to rent one of the fancy dwellings they had built, let alone buy one of them. So they lived in old, cold dwellings, far from the big pyramids, often in flood zones on the banks of the river Nile, as this was the only land that they were able to afford to rent.

[Bilpah, Zilpah and Claire are gathered together, drinking wine out of jam jars.]

BILPAH: Have you seen how extravagant this Pharaoh's pyramid is?! Three bedrooms, a jacuzzi and a home cinema – all for a dead person's grave… and we can't even afford one bedroom for ourselves

ZILPAH: Yeah, the rent is going up and up, but our wages are going down. We're the people who are building the dwellings, not the landlords, who just sit around all day, counting their tithes.

CLAIRE: How ridiculous is it that they think that they 'own' the land! You can't own land, just as we can't own air or oceans. land is a resource that has to be shared by everyone. Worst of all, the pharaoh and his buddies have sectioned off some parts of land so that we're not even allowed to walk on them. Let's reclaim our right to the land

ZILPAH: AMEN SISTER

SCENE 2:

NARRATOR: And so the Israelites began to organise. They held organising meetings cramped within their small dwellings. But as the campaign gathered momentum, they came across a hurdle: they needed larger community spaces to organise in.

BILPAH: There just isn't enough community space for us to use. It has almost all been developed into unaffordable luxury flats and pyramids. And the spaces that are left are too expensive, even to rent for just an hour.

ZILPAH: Not only have they outsourced security so they can use heavy handed force to prevent us from entering the buildings while avoiding accountability, they have also paid for private flood defence, so their houses are protected from the flooding while ours are put at even greater risk.

CLAIRE: Let's bring the security onto our side, they're also low paid workers with poor working conditions. Let's break entry into the newly built flat complex in the city centre and occupy it. It will be a long term, large and accessible meeting space.

BILPAH: YEAH!

SCENE 3:

NARRATOR: At first the Israelites tried a friendly approach to the land-lords. The Israelites explained to the landlords that the land could not be owned by anyone, and landlords had no rights to charge rent for the land. However it became apparent that this strategy wasn't working, so they escalated...

BILPAH: Comrades, we are gathered here today to mark the beginning of our rent strike! This land does not belong to the landlords, it belongs to everyone, and we are here to reclaim it!

ZILPAH: From now on we collectively refuse to pay rent. We do not recognise the landlords' claim on the land, and it was us that built the dwellings, not them.

CLAIRE: We are immigrants in the land of Ancient Egypt, but we have as much right as anyone else to have homes. This land, and the whole earth is for all of us to dwell on and look after.

NARRATOR: And so the Ancient Israelites went on strike, with clear demands and a clear strategy. And they sang this song by Leon Rosselson:

In 1649, to St. George's Hill
A ragged band they called the Diggers came to show the people's will
They defied the landlords, they defied the laws
They were the dispossessed reclaiming what was theirs.

We come in peace, they said, to dig and sow.
We come to work the lands in common and to make the waste ground grow
This earth divided, we will make whole
So it will be a common treasury for all.

The sin of property we do disdain
No man has any right to buy and sell the earth for private gain
By theft and murder they took the land
Now everywhere the walls spring up at their command.

They make the laws to chain us well
The clergy dazzle us with heaven or they damn us into hell
We will not worship the god they serve
The god of greed who feeds the rich while poor folk starve.

We work, we eat together, we need no swords
We will not bow to the master or pay rent to the lords.
Still we are free though we are poor.
You Diggers all stand up for glory, stand up now.

From the men of property the orders came
They sent the hired men and troopers to wipe out the Diggers' claim
Tear down their cottages, destroy their corn.
They were dispersed – but still the vision lingers on.

You poor take courage, you rich take care
This earth was made a common treasury for everyone to share
All things in common, all people one.
We come in peace – the orders came to cut them down

SCENE 4:

NARRATOR: Before long the Ancient Israelites managed to win their rights to the land. And so they dwelled on it, and tended to it as a collective. They ensured that everyone had good quality housing, regardless of where they were born and what work they did. They formed alliances with other oppressed groups in Ancient Egypt, recognising where oppressions intersect, and working to materially liberate all who were oppressed.

They no longer had to spend their days in meaningless jobs building unnecessary luxury apartments for the super rich. Instead they laboured and leisured as they saw fit.

JOSE THE GALILEAN ASKS: How did the rent strike bring about the change? It is surely because each rent striker caused a loss of income to the landlords in the present.

ELIEZAH ANSWERS: Each rent striker did not only bring about a loss of income in the present, they also caused a loss of potential future income. So each rent striker brought about not one, but two plagues to the ruling classes.

SALLY OF THE EAST END CONTRIBUTES: Each rent striker did not bring about two plagues, but 5 plagues. For each strike caused 1) a loss of income in the present, 2) a loss of potential future income, and additionally 3) the devaluation of existing capital, resulting in 4) the inability to generate future capital and 5) the subsequent destruction of the foundation of a capitalist economy

RABBI GEOFFREY CONCLUDES: The plagues of the rent strikers cannot be counted per striker, as the power of the rent strikers should be attributed to their collective organisation which brought about infinite plagues to the ruling classes.

Ten plagues to overthrow Pharaoh

We recite the ten plagues at the seder, spilling a drop of wine for each one. This maintains the communal memory of what to do if ever again we are enslaved by Pharaoh.

דָּם Blood

צְפַרְדֵּעַ Frogs

כִּנִּים Lice

עָרוֹב Wild animals

דֶּבֶר Cattle disease

שְׁחִין Boils

בָּרָד Hail

אַרְבֶּה Locusts

חֹשֶׁךְ Darkness

מַכַּת בְּכוֹרוֹת Death of the first born

Ten plagues to win better terms and conditions of employment

Alternatively, we can read this set of ten plagues which reminds us what to do if we are facing casual or explicit discrimination at work, working in unsafe conditions or not being compensated fairly for our labour.

As you complete each step, spill a drop of wine. The wine represents your bosses' profits in this scenario.

1. ASK THEM NICELY

Call us liberals, but we reckon that asking nicely is always a good start. You could even bring them a beigel. Here are some examples of instances where people have been liberated by asking their oppressors nicely:

OKAY, we didn't find any and we admit that the bosses will probably say no, especially if your demands might mean less money to their shareholders. But they might say yes, so worth a shot anyway – you don't lose anything, just move on quickly if this method doesn't appear to be working.

2. BLOCK THEM ON TWITTER

This is a classic technique, and forms a crucial element of all good strategies. Blocking your boss on Twitter, or even getting into a social media argument avoids face to face confrontation and the passive aggressiveness is 10% sure to get you what you want.

3. WRITE AN OPEN LETTER

This technique, utilised across the Jewish community, but no doubt mastered by Yachad, can be successfully deployed in a range of circumstances. It's so ubiquitous in the Jewish community, the Board of Deputies has even considered making signing an open letter annually a requirement of continued membership of Judaism. Pros: easy Cons: boring

4. WRITE A GUARDIAN OP-ED

Don't let the fact that this technique is popular among liberals put you off. This move is used by George Monbiot and Giles Fraser. We sheepishly put our 'liberal schmiberal' t-shirts away, because we'd be chuffed with a Guardian op-ed, and we think you would be too. Even if it doesn't help you win over your bosses, you can share it on Twitter and get a few more followers, and that's almost as important.

5. GO ON A MARCH AND THROW BEIGELS AT THEM

If this is starting to get a bit too radical for you, then you could go on a static protest at the weekend or evening, though weekday marches are more disruptive and hence more likely to achieve change.

If you want to rack it up a notch, but still want to avoid all the admin that a strike involves, instead of throwing beigels you could steal their beigels. On Pesach you can throw matzah, but you'd have to steal their cinnamon balls, because no one likes motze enough to care if you steal it.

6. GO ON STRIKE FOR A FIXED PERIOD OF TIME

This is fun and can be effective, you get to stand on picket lines, take selfies with the knowledge that whatever happens you'll go back to work and get your payslip at the end of the month. Unfortunately your bosses know this too

7. GO ON INDEFINITE STRIKE

This technique hits your boss where it hurts: their money. By stopping their income and giving them no opportunity to restart the flow of money until they improve your conditions, you have a good chance of achieving your aims.

8. GO ON AN INDEFINITE STRIKE FOR LONGER

See above, but more so.

9. ASK THEM POLITELY

We recommend trying this one more time before you start the revolution, as AA Milne said: 'If the person you are talking to doesn't appear to be listening, be patient. It may simply be that he has a small piece of fluff in his ear.'

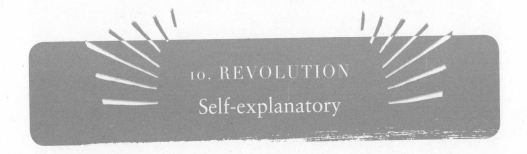

10. REVOLUTION

Self-explanatory

Jewdas adaption of versions by Geoff Berner
and Zalmen Mlotek

In ale gasn vu men geyt
Hert men zabostovkes.
Yinglekh, meydlekh, kind un keyt
Shmuesn fun pribovkes.
Genug shoyn brider horeven,
Genug shoyn borgn layen,
Makht a zabostovke,
Lomir brider zikh bafrayen!

Brider un shvester,
Lumir zikh gehn di hent,
Lomir Nikolaykelen tsebrekhn di vent!

Hey, hey, daloy politsey!
Daloy samederzhavyets v'rasey!
Out of your houses and in to the streets
Everybody say FUCK THE POLICE

Brider un shvester, lomir zikh nit irtsn,
Lomir Nikolaykelen di yorelekh farkirtsn!
Hey, hey, daloy Theresa May!
Daloy samederzhavyets UK
Out of your houses and in to the streets
Everybody say FUCK THE TORIES

Nekhtn hot er gefirt a vegele mit mist,
Haynt is er gevorn a kapitalist!
Hey, hey, daloy politsey!
Daloy samederzhavyets Turkey!
Out of your houses and in to the streets
Everybody say FUCK THE ARMIES

Brider un shvester, lomir geyn tsuzamen,
Lomir Nikolaykelen bagrobn mit der mamen!
Hey, hey, daloy politsey!
Daloy samederzhavyets USA!
Out of your houses and in to the streets
Everybody say FUCK THE NAZIS

Kozakn, zhandarrnen, arop fun di ferd!
Der rusisher keyser ligt shoyn in dr'erd!
Hey, hey Daloy politsey
It means the same thing now as yesterday.
Out of your houses, into the streets
Everybody say 'Fuck the police!'

Dayeinu

It is a Sephardic tradition to hit each other on the head with spring onions while singing dayeinu. This tradition is said to originate from an Ancient Israelite practice. Once they left Ancient Egypt and were wandering the desert, if they expressed any sentiments of returning to ancient Egypt, they would rapidly be hit on the head with a spring onion, to get rid of the offending thoughts.

Voltn mir nor fun Mitsrayim
Gliklekh oisgeleyzt gevorn
Nor der yam zikh nit geshpoltn
- Dayeinu

If we had only been deliverd from Egypt, but the sea had not split… Dayeinu

Volt der yam zikh shoyn geshpoltn
Nor im durkhgeyn in der trukn,
Volt undz demolt nit gegoltn
- Dayenu.

If the sea had split and we had only come out dry… Dayeinu

Voltn mir im shoyn ariber
Nit gekent nor iberkumen,
Fertsik yor in groysn midber
- Dayeinu

If we had made it over, only to spend 40 years in the wilderness… Dayeinu

Voltn mir di fertsik yor shoyn
In dem midber durkhgekumen
Un keyn man dort nit gefunen
- Dayeinu

If we had spent 40 years in the desert and found no life there… Dayeinu

Voltn mir dort man gefunen,
Nor dem shabes nit bakumen,
Un tsum Sinay nit gekumen …
Dayeinu

If we had found life there but not received shabbat… Dayeinu

Second Cup

A BLESSING FOR STRANGERS

Throughout the Torah, we are commanded to be good to strangers, because we were strangers in the land of Egypt. Tonight is all about remembering that history, of what it is to be an outsider, an other in a narrow place and the struggle to be liberated from persecution, exploitation and narrow mindedness. We drink this glass of wine in solidarity with migrants who are still wandering and trying to find a place they can call home and be free. We drink also in solidarity with all strangers, with all the weirdos at our own table, and in defiance of what society tells us is normal and acceptable.

ברוּךְ אַתָּה יי אֱלֹהֵינוּ מֶלֶךְ הָעוֹלָם
בּוֹרֵא פְּרִי הַגָּפֶן

Baruch atah A-donay, Elo-heinu Melech Ha'Olam borei pri hagafen.

Blessed are You Adonai, our God, Ruler of the universe, Who creates the fruit of the vine

Hand washing
Rachtzah רחצה

Why do we wash our hands a second time? Didn't we just do this already? The reason for the second washing transcends our collective dedication to personal hygiene. Rather it is to wash off the effects of patriarchal erasure and the erasures that result from all other oppressive systems. How do we know this is true? Because when our ancestors were getting hopelessly lost in the desert, the washing basin used in the Tabernacle, our handy portable shrine, was made from the mirrors of the Tzovot. Who were the Tzovot, you might ask? And why didn't I learn about them in Cheder? The Tzovot were women who served in an official capacity at the gateway to the Tabernacle and later at the gateways to other holy shrines, i.e. priestesses! See Exodus 38.

As we wash our hands, we remember the sacred work of women and those of other marginalised genders, so often rendered invisible, and we uplift their stories for the sake of collective liberation.

ברוכה את שכינה אלוהינו רוח העולם, אשר קדשתנו במצותיה רצותנו על נטילת ידיים

Berucha at Shekhinah, Eloteinu Ruach Ha'Olam, asher kidshatnu bemitzvoteha v'tzivatnu al netilat yadayim.

Blessed are You, Shekhinah Our Goddess, who has given us many sacred works to do, including cleansing ourselves of ideas which oppress us and others, and making visible that which has been erased.

Pinkwashing

Why does the Israeli state desperately try to market itself as LGBT-friendly, progressive and inclusive? Don't they abuse and ignore the human rights of Palestinians on a regular basis? The reason for this is to use a record on LGBT rights (that is in reality quite debatable) to cynically rebrand Israel as a modern state, not in keeping with its 'savage' neighbours and further the 'only democracy in the Middle East™' narrative. Israel cannot be pro-LGBT while gay Palestinians are shot while protesting and trans Palestinians' houses are demolished. For Israel, the LGBT community is a shield with which to fend off attacks from the Western world and behind which to hide their oppressive regime.

You can eat an olive from the seder plate if you wish and recite this prayer:

אֵל מָלֵא רַחֲמִים וּמַתִּיר אֲסוּרִים
מַבְקִיעַ יַמִּים וּפוֹרֵץ גְּדֵרוֹת:
תְּקַע בְּשׁוֹפָר גָּדוֹל לְחֵרוּתֵנוּ
וְשָׂא נֵס לְקַבֵּץ גָּלֻיּוֹתֵינוּ
וְקַבְּצֵנוּ יַחַד מְהֵרָה מֵאַרְבַּע כַּנְפוֹת הָאָרֶץ לְאַרְצֵנוּ
הֲשִׁיבֵם יהוה אַרְצָה: וְיָשִׁיבוּ
בְּרוּכִים הֵם: בְּצֵאתָם וּבְשׁוּבָם
דְּרוֹר יִקְרָא: וְיִגַּל כַּמַּיִם מִשְׁפָּט עַל יְרוּשָׁלַיִם
וּצְדָקָ כְּנַחַל אֵיתָן לְעַזָּה

El male rachamim u'metir asurim
Mavkia yamim u'porets gderot:
Teka b'shofar gadol l'cherutenu
V'sa nes lekabets galyuteinu
U'kabtsenu yachad mehera mi arba knefot ha'arets le artsenu
Hashivam Adonai artsa: v'yashivu
Bruchim hem: be tse'etam u'be shuvam
Dror yikra: v'yigal ka mayim mishpat al yerushalayim
V'tsedek ke nachal eitan l'aza

God full of mercy who releases prisoners
Divides seas and breaches barriers:
Sound a big shofar for our liberty
And carry out a miracle to gather in our exile
And gather us in quickly from the four corners of the earth to the land
Return them to the land Adonai: and they will return
Blessed are they: in their expulsion and in their return
Cry freedom: let judgement roll like a wave upon Jerusalem
And justice like a mighty stream to Gaza

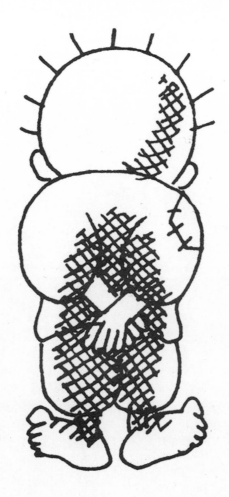

This illustration by Naji al-Ali is called Handala. 'Handala was born ten years old, and he will always be ten years old. At that age, I left my homeland, and when he returns, Handala will still be ten, and then he will start growing up. The laws of nature do not apply to him. He is unique. Things will become normal again when the homeland returns.

'I presented him to the poor and named him Handala as a symbol of bitterness. At first, he was a Palestinian child, but his consciousness developed to have a national and then a global and human horizon. He is a simple yet tough child, and this is why people adopted him and felt that he represents their consciousness.'

Seder plate

ORANGE

There are many midrashim to explain how the orange came to be on the seder plate at lefty seders. Whether it symbolises the inclusion of women or LGBT+ people, the result is the same: the orange is not only a new addition to the seder plate, but a large, clunky, bright orange one at that. It does not fit in, but we don't just tolerate it and include it, we celebrate it.

MOTZE

This is the bread of affliction. When the Israelites were fleeing Egypt they didn't have time to lounge around waiting for the bread to rise. So instead they cooked the dough pretty much as soon as they had made it, which resulted in flat breads – motze.

The flatness of the motze also represents our vision for the distribution of power and resources in society, we want people to be on the same level.

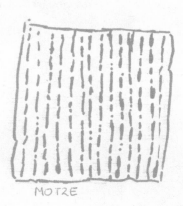

MOTZE

EGG

The egg symbolises new life. The egg also represents antifascism. Wherever you come from, whatever you look like, we all came from eggs.

SALT WATER

The salt water represents the tears of the Israelites, and reminds us of their suffering. It also reminds us of the need to salt our workplaces and communities, so those who are oppressed today can win liberation.

CHAROSET

The charoset represents the mortar with which the Israelites built the pyramids.

KARPAS

(see page 45 for full explanation)

MAROR

Maror is the bitter herbs. They represent the bitterness that our ancestors endured when they were slaves in Egypt.

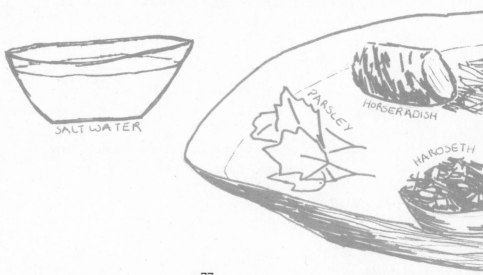

ANTICAPITALIST BEETROOT

Last year the Jewdas anticapitalist beetroot that we had on our seder plate instead of the shank bone was made famous by the Daily Mail. As a result we sold the anticapitalist beetroot online, and it is now no longer available or anticapitalist.

You may wish to revert to the traditional shank bone which represents the temptation of idolatry and therefore consumer capitalism, which we put on the seder plate to remind us that it's gross. If you don't want a yucky bone on your seder plate, then please pick another root vegetable such as the antifascist carrot, the anti-fracking fennel or the anarcho potato.

Please raise your chosen symbolic food in the air and shake it like a lulav, march to your nearest bank and throw it through the window and shout

fuck capitalism.

(the world is literally gonna die by 2040, we don't have time to fuck around this year)

Before the meal

MOTZI, MOTZE מוציא מצה

Hold the motze up and recite:

בָּרוּךְ אַתָּה ה', אֱלֹהֵינוּ רוח הָעוֹלָם, אֲשֶׁר קִדְּשָׁנוּ בְּמִצְוֹתָיו
וְצִוָּנוּ עַל אֲכִילַת מַצָּה

Baruch atah Adonai eloheinu ru'akh ha'olam asher kidshanu b'mitzvotav
v'tzivanu al achilat motze

Blessed are You, Spirit of the Earth, Holder of the Universe, who has sanctified
us with Your commandments and has commanded us on the eating of matsa.

MAROR מרור

Dip the maror in the charoset and recite:

ברוכה את שכינה אלוהינו רוח העולם אשר קדשתנו במצותיה
וצותנו על אכילת מרור

Brukha at Shekhina eloheinu ru'akh ha'olam asher kidshatnu bmitzovoteiha
vitzivatnu al achilat maror

Blessed are You, Mysterious God, transcender of time, who has sanctified us
with Her commandments and has commanded us on the eating of marror.

KOREICH כורך

*Now make a sandwich with some charoset and maror contained within two
pieces of motze.*

ברוכה את שכינה, אלוהינו רוח העולם, אשר קדשתנו במצותיה
וצותנו על אכילת סנדוויץ'

Baruch atah Adonai eloheinu melekh haolam asher kidshanu bmitzovotav
vitzivanu al achilat sandwich

Blessed are you God, keeper of the world who sanctified us with Her
commandments and who has commanded us on the eating of sandwiches

SHULCHAN OREICH שלחן עור

Partake in the repast

Afikomen
Tzafun

Now is the time for the afikomen hunt. Traditionally the younger participants at the seder take part, and seek out the afikomen. Afikomen is the dessert, and is essential to end the seder.

Once they have found the afikomen, it is our tradition that they hold the gathering to ransom by demanding payment for afikomen. This is because Hashem wants us to teach our children the principles of organising at a young age.

A tradition which was popularised in the Jewish East End at the turn of the century was to break into the houses of the high up Jewish establishment people to take their afikomen and refuse to give it back until they give in to your demands which ranged from ending the anti-immigration lobbying that the Jewish establishment engaged with at the time to asking them to improve the quality of kiddushes across shuls (some things never change).

More recently Geoffrey planned to break into Bibi's house on seder night to demand that there is an equal right of return for Palestinians and Jews. Unfortunately Geoffrey was held up by the border guards at Ben Gurion and missed the seder.

Distribute the afikomen and eat it.

Tips for children on negotiating:

1. We suggest all the children at the seder organise themselves into a collective.

2. Then collectively negotiate for the best deal.

3. Demand fair wages for all household chores. Remember housework is work.

Bareich ברך

Brich rachamana
Malka D'alma
M'arei
D'hai pita

Oh God prepare me
To be a revolutionary
Bold and tender
Tried and true
And with each other
We'll build another
World together
For me and you

Lyrics by Margot Seigle

bendigamos

SPANISH:	ENGLISH:
Bendigamos	Let us bless
Bendigamos al Altísimo,	Let us bless the Most High
Al Señor que nos crió,	The Lord who raised us,
Démosle agradecimiento	Let us give him thanks
Por los bienes que nos dió.	For the good things which he gave us.
Alabado sea su Santo Nombre,	Praised be his Holy Name,
Porque siempre nos apiadó.	Because he always took pity on us.
Load al Señor que es bueno,	Praise the Lord, for he is good,
Que para siempre su merced.	For his mercy is everlasting.
Bendigamos al Altísimo,	Let us bless the Most High
Por su Ley primeramente,	First for his Law,
Que liga a nuestra raza	Which binds our race
Con el cielo continuamente,	With heaven continually,
Alabado sea su Santo Nombre,	Praised be his Holy Name,
Porque siempre nos apiadó.	Because he always took pity on us.
Load al Senor que es bueno,	Praise the Lord, for he is good,
Que para siempre su merced.	For his mercy is everlasting.
Bendigamos al Altísimo,	Let us bless the Most High,
Por el pan segundamente,	Secondly for the bread
Y también por los manjares	And also for the food
Que comimos juntamente.	Which we eat together.
Pues comimos y bebimos alegremente	For we have eaten and drunk happily
Su merced nunca nos faltó.	His mercy has never failed us.
Load al Señor que es bueno,	Praise the Lord, for he is good,
Que para siempre su merced.	For his mercy is everlasting.
Bendita sea la casa esta,	Blessed be this house,
El hogar de su presencia,	The home of his presence,
Donde guardamos su fiesta,	Where we keep his feast,
Con alegría y permanencia.	With happiness and permanence.
Alabado sea su Santo Nombre,	Praised be his Holy Name,
Porque siempre nos apiadó.	Because he always took pity on us.
Load al Señor que es bueno,	Praise the Lord, for he is good,
Que para siempre su merced.	For his mercy is everlasting.

Third cup

We've made it this far, the seder's almost done. And no one's mentioned the Holocaust yet.

If someone at your seder has already mentioned the Holocaust, you've lost the seder. Do not pass go, do not take a selfie with Jeremy Corbyn. Put down the fucking beetroot and start the whole thing again from the beginning, and this time don't mention the Holocaust until you get to this cup of wine.

As Pesach reminds us, Jewish history is full of stories of persecution and liberation. It is a heritage of survival, resilience and resistance. But trauma cannot be healed quickly, even by finding meaning in stories of survival. After we were liberated from Egypt, we had to wander in the desert for 40 years before reaching the promised land, so that a generation would pass and new foundations would be laid by people no longer carrying the trauma of slavery. In our modern, capitalist society, there is neither the time nor the space to wander in the wilderness. The history that is unfolding around us today is one in which the traumas of the twentieth century, far from healed, are carried forward and inflicted on other vulnerable peoples.

We raise this third cup of wine in solidarity with all peoples still suffering under persecution and oppression, and commit to stand with them in their struggles. We celebrate our own survival, and we also pray for the time and the space to heal from our collective traumas.

בְּרוּכָה אָת יה אֱלֹהֵינוּ רוּחַ הָעוֹלָם בּוֹרֵאת פְּרִי הַגֶּפֶן

B'rukha At Yah Eloheynu Ruakh ha'olam boreyt p'ri hagofen

You are blessed, Our God, Spirit of the World,
who creates the fruit of the vine

Hallel הלל

Ozi v'zimrat Yah vay'hi li lishuah

עָזִּי וְזִמְרָת יָהּ וַיְהִי לִי לִישׁוּעָה

If I had the strength
I would run through the streets
And I would cry out peace, peace, peace

Volt ikh gehat koyekh,
Volt ikh gelofn in di gasn,
Volt ikh geshrign sholem, sholem, sholem

וואָלט איך געהאַט כּח

וואָלט איך געלאָפֿן אין די גאַסן

וואָלט איך געשריגן שלום, שלום, שלום

PSALM 92: SONG AFTER REVOLUTION BY RABBI BRANT ROSEN

tonight we raise the cup,
tomorrow we'll breathe deeply
and dwell in a world
without borders, without limit
in space or in time,
a world beyond wealth or scarcity,
a world where there is nothing
for us to do but to be.

they said this day would never come,
yet here we are:
the surging waters have receded,
there is no oppressor, no oppressed,
no power but the one
coursing through every living
breathing satiated soul.

memories of past battles fading
like dry grass in the warm sun,
no more talk of enemies and
strategies,

no more illusions, no more dreams,
only
this eternal moment of victory
to celebrate and savour the world
as we always knew it could be.

see how the justice we planted in the
deep
dark soil now soars impossibly sky-
ward,
rising up like a palm tree,
like a cedar, flourishing forever
ever swaying, ever bending
but never breaking.

so tonight we raise the cup,
tomorrow we'll breathe deeply
to savour a world recreated,
and when the sun sets once again
we continue the struggle.

ELIJAH'S CUP

(open the door to see if Elijah is outside, and raise Elijah's cup)

We are taught that Elijah will come just before the coming of the messianic age (read: revolution) to forewarn us. This seems a bit passive to us, as we tend to believe that ha'olam haba will come about by a lot of organising, campaigning and working.

So, if Elijah does turn up we will celebrate, not because the ha'olam haba will be any closer (that is in our hands anyway), but because we'll have an extra person on board to help us organise.

Raise the cup: To the end of capitalism, to renationalisation of many things, to communism, to the future

MIRIAM'S CUP

We raise a cup to Miriam and to all the women and non-binary people who have been silenced by our traditions. With this cup we acknowledge their work in building our traditions and commit to telling their stories.

Raise the cup: To all the great women and non-binary people who wove our past, create our present and who build for tomorrow

GEOFFREY'S CUP

We raise a cup to our struggle with the Jewish establishment, to smashing the hierarchies within anglo-Jewry, to making liberal Zionists feel uncomfortable. With this cup we honour all the mischief that we have made and all the mischief that we will make.

Raise the cup: To diasporism, to heresy, to singing out of time and out of tune, to communal broiges, (insert your own here)

To Geoffrey!

Fourth cup

A BLESSING FOR FREEDOM

Whether you're on your fourth cup of wine or your fourth cup of tea, hopefully you are feeling pretty relaxed. During our Seder, we've mentioned so many people who currently and historically are still struggling for freedom. And there are so many more we haven't had space to mention. Thinking about the pain and suffering in the world, about how few people in it are actually really free, is exhausting, and itself can become a prison. As we raise this glass, we allow ourselves a moment of freedom from the constant struggle, a moment to celebrate everything that has already been achieved, even though there is still so much more to be done.

בְּרוּכָה אַתְּ יה אֱלֹהֵינוּ רוּחַ
הָעוֹלָם בּוֹרֵאת פְּרִי הַגֶּפֶן

B'rukha At Yah Eloheynu Ruakh ha'olam boreyt p'ri hagofen

You are blessed, Our God, Spirit of the World,
who creates the fruit of the vine

More Songs

'CHAD GADYA, CHAD GADYA.

D'zabin aba bitrei zuzei,
chad gadya, chad gadya.

V'ata shunra v'achlah l'gadya,
d'zabin aba bitrei zuzei,
chad gadya, chad gadya.

V'ata chalba v'nashach l'shunrah,
d'achlah l'gadya,
d'zabin aba bitrei zuzei,
chad gadya, chad gadya.

V'ata chutra v'hika l'chalba,
d'nashach l'shunrah,
d'achlah l'gadya,
d'zabin aba bitrei zuzei,
chad gadya, chad gadya.

V'ata nura v'saraf l'chutra,
d'hikah l'chalba,
d'nashach l'shunrah,
d'achlah l'gadya,
d'zabin aba bitrei zuzei,
chad gadya, chad gadya.

V'ata maya v'chava l'nura,
d'saraf l'chutra,
d'hikah l'chalba,
d'nashach l'shunrah,
d'achlah l'gadya,
d'zabin aba bitrei zuzei,
chad gadya, chad gadya.

V'ata tora v'shatah l'maya,
d'chava l'nura,
d'saraf l'chutra,
d'hikah l'chalba,
d'nashach l'shunrah,
d'achlah l'gadya,
d'zabin aba bitrei zuzei,
chad gadya, chad gadya.

V'ata hashocheit v'shachat l'tora,
d'shata l'maya,
d'chava l'nura,
d'saraf l'chutra,
d'hikah l'chalba,
d'nashach l'shunrah,
d'achlah l'gadya,
d'zabin aba bitrei zuzei,
chad gadya, chad gadya.
V'ata malach hamavet v'shachat l'shocheit,
d'shachat l'tora,
d'shata l'maya,
d'chava l'nura,
d'saraf l'chutra,
d'hikah l'chalba,
d'nashach l'shunrah,
d'achlah l'gadya,
d'zabin aba bitrei zuzei,
chad gadya, chad gadya.

V'ata Hakodesh Baruch Hu v'shachat l'malach hamavet,
d'shachat l'shocheit,
d'shachat l'tora,
d'shata l'maya,
d'chava l'nura,
d'saraf l'chutra,
d'hikah l'chalba,
d'nashach l'shunrah,
d'achlah l'gadya,
d'zabin aba bitrei zuzei,
chad gadya, chad gadya.

BELLA CIAO

Yiddish version by respected comrade and Yiddishist
Barry Davis who passed away in 2017

Una mattina mi son svegliato	A sheyn frimorgn hob ikh ge**khapt** zikh
O bella ciao, bella ciao, bella ciao ciao ciao	Bella ciao! Bella ciao! Bella ciao ciao ciao!
Una mattina mi son svegliato	A sheyn fri**morgn** hob ikh ge**khapt** zikh
Eo ho trovato l'invasor	Un der **soyne** shteyt arum
O partigiano porta mi via	A parti**zan**er, nem mikh a**vek** mit,
O bella ciao, bella ciao, bella ciao ciao ciao	Bella ciao! Bella ciao! Bella ciao ciao ciao!
O partigiano porta mi via	A parti**zan**er, nem mikh a**vek** mit,
Che mi sento di morir	Vayl tsu **shtar**bn bin ikh greyt
E se io muoio da partigiano	Un az ikh **shtarb** vi partizaner
O bella ciao, bella ciao, bella ciao ciao ciao	Bella ciao! Bella ciao! Bella ciao ciao ciao!
E se io muoio da partigiano	Un az ikh **shtarb** vi partizaner
Tu mi devi seppellir	Mustu **mikh** makaber zayn
Mi seppellire lassù in montagna	**Bagrob** mik in berg di **hoykhe**
O bella ciao, bella ciao, bella ciao ciao ciao	Bella ciao! Bella ciao! Bella ciao ciao ciao!
Mi seppellire lassù in montagna	**Bagrob** mik in berg di **hoykhe**
Sotto l'ombra di un bel fiore	Dem kevyer a **kveyt** farshotenem
E le genti che passeranno	Un az di **men**tshn veln far**bay**geyen
O bella ciao, bella ciao, bella ciao ciao ciao	Bella ciao! Bella ciao! Bella ciao ciao ciao!
E le genti che passeranno	Un az di **men**tshn veln far**bay**geyen
Mi diranno: "Che bel fior"	Veln zey **zogn** "a sheyner **blum**"
È questo il fiore del partigiano	"Es iz di **blum** fun partisa**nen**"
O bella ciao, bella ciao, bella ciao ciao ciao	Bella ciao! Bella ciao! Bella ciao ciao ciao!
È questo il fiore del partigiano	"Es iz di **blum** fun partisanen"
Morto per la libertà	A korbn far undser **kheyrus**

WHO KNOWS ONE?

Who knows one? I know one: one humankind is here in the world.

Who knows two? I know two: in two parts is humankind divided:
poor and rich.

Who knows three? I know three: the Christian Trinity darkens the world.

Who knows four? I know four: the four basics rule work.

Who knows five? I know five: Capital controls all five continents.

Who knows six? I know six: six days of the week a worker becomes
besmirched.

Who knows seven? I know seven: the rich person counts seven
days a week as Holiday.

Who knows eight? I know eight: from eight days on, a little boy
already suffers because of religion.

Who knows nine? I know nine: Nine months to work three months
closer to death.

Who knows ten? I know ten: from ten commandments came the 613 mitsvot.

Who knows eleven? I know eleven: only rabbis and idlers can compare eleven
merchants with eleven stars.

Who knows twelve? I know twelve: twelve holes are in a dozen bagels,
and this is opposed to the twelve tribes.

Who knows thirteen? I know thirteen: to thirteen thousand atheists is
the Capitalist system useless!

From the 1900 Bund Haggadah - full citation found on Page 55

חֲסַל סִדּוּר פֶּסַח כְּהִלְכָתוֹ, כְּכָל מִשְׁפָּטוֹ וְחֻקָּתוֹ.
כַּאֲשֶׁר זָכִינוּ לְסַדֵּר אוֹתוֹ. כֵּן נִזְכֶּה לַעֲשׂוֹתוֹ

Nirtzah: Meaning: We will want, we will run, or, we have satisfied. The seder has ended, but our desire has not. We want something more. We want this work we did now to spill out into the real world, beyond the space of Seder. The Nirtzah begins with the word חֲסַל *(chasal).*

And together we chant:

Chasal!

It's over! That's that!

Hearkening back to the Aramaic earlier in the haggadah, with *ha lachmah anya*, this is the bread of affliction, we bookend our seder with Aramaic, a language of diaspora, but this time we hope for something new. We go from inviting in to spreading out, from inviting the needy into our homes, to sharing the wealth out.

So we've finished it, and we chant out loud:

According to Halachah, or according to no rules at all.

According to all kinds of Jewish laws we 'forgot' to follow.

As we merited to 'seder' it.

Thus may we merit to do it!

Nirtzah נרצה

But what kind of action?

[Growing up, when we arrived at Nirtzah, the final step of the Passover seder, my dad would always announce: Chabad do not do Nirtzah. The seder is never-ending. It is never concluded. We go out from tonight's Seder into the world, without needing to conclude it.]

But even for Chabad the next unfortunate bit could not be excised. So, we recite together one of the below versions, according to the custom of the community:

Nirtzah I

This version is recited by communities that really dislike the whole Jerusalem thing, but still feel like they have to say it rather than offending the one Zionist at the table.

לְשָׁנָה הַבָּאָה בִּירוּשָׁלָיִם

**Lishana haba'ah b'yerushalaim
Next year in... Jerusalem??**

The place we have always desired and run to. Jerusalem!

Nirtzah II

This version was written especially for this haggadah.

לְשָׁנָה הַבָּאָה בִּירוּשָׁלָיִם

Lishana haba'ah b'yerushalaim to bring new change to Jerusalem.

(Lishanah - to change, habaah - the coming, or the next).

CHANGE THE COMING TO JERUSALEM!!

Nirtzah III

to be recited only if you're in Sheffield

Next year, a rebuilt Sheffield, a Sheffield of wisdom. A Sheffield built or unbuilt, on compassion and not on oppression.

If you are Breslov, you might not go next year to Jerusalem – you might be journeying to Uman. And if you're Lisensk, which is a type of chossid that no longer exists, but maybe you'll make pilgrimage to Lisensk – the Jerusalem of Eastern Europe.

For a *chossid*, Jerusalem is not a geographical place, but the heart, the center of being...

For example, Elimelekh of Lisensk writes that the nachalah, inheritance, given to us, is not the land, but the *Nachal Hashem*, the upper river that we connect with to draw forth influence to change the world.

The journey or pilgrimage is not to Jerusalem but to the Rebbe.

So when we say next year in Jerusalem, we are asking for a place that is whole and inherited, a place close to our hearts, from which we can act and freely be our most radical selves.

Next year in Lisensk!

By which we mean, and we say all together, regardless of our custom:

next year in ~~Golders Green~~ Sheffield!

The Passover seder has been completed, according to all its rules and regulations which, as devotees of Rav Geoffrey, we have dutifully satirised, dissolved, lampooned, re-written and re-made for the sake of collective liberation.

Just as we merited this gathering, so may we and all who inhabit this Earth merit to live in a world in which all systems of oppression have been dissolved. Shekhinah, raise us up in our collective struggle.

Bring near the day when all of Your people feel rooted enough to rejoice in Diaspora, having built solidarity with one another and all the peoples of the Earth.

Diasbara

NO BORDERS NO BORDERS

We are very excited to present this
issue of Diasbara, a magazine for
diasporist Jews.

Diasporism isn't just another word
for non or anti-Zionism. While
non-Zionism is about fighting the
values and ideas that we don't hold,
diasporism is about living the values
that we do hold.

It is about learning, struggling,
celebrating and mourning for Jewish
communities all over the world. Read
on to find out more....

Getting Birthwrong right

By all measures* this year's birthwrong trip to Amsterdam has been highly successful, proving its continued relevance and importance to diasporist Jews. It differs from Birthright not just in location, but in its entire philosophy.

For Birthwrongniks, the trip isn't a holiday. It is a diasporist study trip. Birthwrongniks take a break from their own organising to learn about the organising and activism of communities in other places. A highlight of all Birthwrong trips is connecting with local lefty-Jewish communities, so we can share our ideas and experiences and also be assured to have a homely Shabbes table to be welcomed to. For one participant, sharing Shabbes dinner with the local community in Birthwrong Marseille in 2017 was particularly significant, as she has a letter (see fig A) which shows her great great grandmother shared Friday night dinner with the local Jewish lefties in Marseille on Birthwrong 1910!

Birthwrong isn't just about discovering different diaspora Jewish communities. It is also a chance to learn more about our own history and community. The trips to the museum of resistance in Birthwrong Amsterdam and to Andalusia in Birthwrong Spain brought to light the stories of our ancestors that had been papered over by the Zionist narrative of Jewish history.

Birthwrong goes far beyond creating an alternative Birthright, instead it operates within a different paradigm entirely. Letter B from Birthwrong in the 1950s contains the dreams of its writer, Miryam, inspired by what she saw, heard and ate on Birthwrong. Her dream of luxury communism and a world without borders are shared by people across the world and throughout time.

There are many reasons why increasing numbers of Jews are rejecting Birthright: for some it is a profound dislike of Jewish ethno-nationalism, for others it is simply not worth travelling half-way across the world to pull now that Jewish dating apps exist. Whatever the reasons it is clear that Birthwrong is getting it right.

---

* Measures include: quality and quantity of food, relevance of activities, depth of political education and 'fun'

Figure A:

Figure B:

Appeal from American Friends of Jewdas

Every day in the States, we hear more heartbreaking news of Jewdas halutzim suffering in Europe. These brave Jews are eking out a radical Jewish existence in lands which are completely sparse and deserted.

They have returned to their roots, reviving radical lefty Jewish life. But it is not easy. They are constantly oppressed by capitalism, high rents and boring rabbis.

They need our help. With our help Jewdas will be able to make the desert bloom and bring moshiach sooner.

Guest column – from Treyf!

Devoted Treyf fans are well aware that we spend a lot of time focusing on the Jewish media landscape. But in addition to critiquing, grimacing, and groaning in response to the news of the day, we also spotlight older Jewish media with the hope of giving today's generation a glimpse of the glory days of the Jewish press.

Our inbox is usually reserved for hate mail and longly worded critiques, but we recently received an encrypted email from a contact in deep cover within the bowels of an unnamed Zionist organisation. Along with warm militant greetings and an invitation to a 5780 Yom Kippur ball, the message contained a groundbreaking interview that sheds light on the media our ancestors consumed. Our contact, who works in the archives, knew that we were the only Jewish podcast brave enough to release this information to the public.

https://treyfpodcast.wordpress.com/

> Brace yourself! What you are about to read is an unedited transcript of a recording that has never been shared outside of the unidentified organisation's secret bunker.

Treyf image by Cee Lavery

MITZRAYIM, AROUND 1500 BCE

INARA: Hello comrade! I'm in town for the Hittite Chronicle, investigating the contemporary Jewish experience under Pharoah.

ESTHER: Ach, being a Jew under Pharaoh is no dip in the Nile!

INARA: But Phar-ox News always says that it's great for business...

ESTHER: Good business for who?! That's what you get for trusting the Pharonic-controlled media. If you want to know about the streets of Mitzrayim, you have to read the publications of the people.

INARA: Oh, I didn't realize that there were Jewish publications here. Are there any you'd recommend?

ESTHER: Well, it depends on your political persuasion and how you feel about being fed to crocodiles.

INARA: Just give it to me straight.

ESTHER: There's no better place to start than with the **Jewish Daily Backward**. They used to be progressive but they started writing in Coptic and now mostly do those "10 Reasons Pharoah's Good for the Jews" type of stories. If you want 'balanced' coverage–say, a Jewish labourer debating one of Pharoah's PR people–this is the scroll for you.

INARA: Sounds like a confused newsroom to me.

ESTHER: You don't know the half of it. Next, you have the **JPA, the Jewish Pictographic Agency**. It mostly consists of press releases from pro-Pharoah groups packaged as news. The other scrolls copy a lot of their stories to fill their pages.

INARA: Huh, in the Hittite Kingdom that's called plagiarism.

ESTHER: Well, here it's called business! Welcome to Mitzrayim. Then there's The Tablet, one of the most mocked scrolls on the World Wide Well. They get financed by Jewish Pharoah supporters, you couldn't find bigger proponents of the Pithom and Ramses development if you tried! Last year they had a great review of Rosa's new art scroll but didn't ever mention her opposition to Pharoah.

INARA: Wow, are all the Jewish newspapyruses so right wing?

ESTHER: Oh if those are too reactionary for you, I won't even get into all the scrolls with editors who wear "Make Mitzrayim Great Again" linens. There used to be more revolutionary vigour. The **Free Voice of Labour** once had a scroll subscription of nearly 20,000! Emma Gold's speeches were published in there, I think I still have a few old copies somewhere...

INARA: What happened?

ESTHER: There just isn't the same sympathy for political anarchism among the Jews these days. Especially with Pharoah's no-shirts circulating their counterfeit mouthpiece 'The Voice of Free Labor!'

INARA: And there's nothing comparable to that now?

ESTHER: It's complicated. Have you ever taken water from the World Wide Well? The youth carve ironic hieroglyphs into it for each other to read and I've been told they've been getting quite radical! I've also heard that if you lean down the well, you can even hear something called a sodcast.

INARA: Interesting... so they don't use scrolls anymore?

ESTHER: There's still the Jewish Currents of the Nile who've been writing scrolls since the mid-40s (1446 BCE). Back then, it was run by secular Communists but Pharonic repression and more comfortable living huts changed its direction. Some of the Well kids actually took it over recently. They're a little less secular and a little less Communist but times have changed and they seem to grasp that.

INARA: I think I get the picture. So do you only sell scrolls or do you write them too?

ESTHER: Oh, I got out of the newspapyrus game; it's a bad scene these days. I've been working on a fantasy scroll for a while though. It's about these plagues that hit Pharoah. I was actually working on a chapter this morning where – get this – the sea splits in half!

INARA: I'd love to read a copy of that when you're done. I can already imagine a sequel!

Towards a Jewish Pacifism

Historiography is always political. The right to write the history books, to set the narrative, to fix the canonical account is always claimed by the victors and bitterly contested by their opponents. Nowhere is this more true than in the field of Jewish history. The mainstream account, emanating from the Zionist movement has achieved almost total hegemony. From its most outlandish claims, talking of Abraham having made the first aliyah, claiming the land was essentially barren and void between 70 CE and 1948, to more subtle and insidious propaganda, such as presenting the entirety of diaspora existence as negative and essentialising a difference between Jews and others (particularly Muslims) to imply that they will never be able to live together without separation, the mainstream account has become the dominant narrative. This dominance has been aggressively enforced, anyone who contests it is at best ignored and at worst denounced by means of the usual assimilationist/self-hating insults. It may be, as Art Nelsen recently suggested, that Zionists are so defensive because their case is so dubious.

One of the strongest idols of Zionist/mainstream Jewish opinion is of the importance of military strength, and the need for Jews to be strong and able to fight their enemies. A whole range of role models from the tradition are dragged up to support this viewpoint, usually figures like Samson, King David and the Macabees and occasions like Masada and the Bar Kochba Revolt. These, of course were not the key heroes of rabbinic thought, and most violence in biblical tradition was either explained away as being only possible at that time, or actually condemned by the rabbis, sometimes subtly and sometimes overtly. The Macabees were written out of the Channukah story. A haftarah reading allotted for shabbat channukah, containing the lines 'not by might and not by power', while the Masada martyrs were traditionally considered grossly irresponsible. The story largely forgotten. It is revealing, that when an Israeli Kibbutz wanted to call itself Masada, no one knew how to spell it in Hebrew. Daniel Boyarin, in his book Unheroic Conduct, about Judaism and masculinity, points out that in the haggadah,

the wise son was regularly depicted as a scholar and the wicked son a strongman. This is not reversed until a Palmach haggadah of 1948 illustrated the wise son as a haganah fighter. The vast majority of traditional Judaism venerated the Jacob, the stereotypical gentle, scholarly Jew, over Esau, seen as the epitome of empire and violence, a model to be avoided at all costs.

In this context the figure of Rabbi Aaron Samuel Tamaret occupies a strange position. As a radical pacifist, he is, according to the mainstream account, a total anomaly, a freak in Jewish history, the exception that proves the rule. According to the 'counertcultural' narrative offered above, he may be in direct continuation of a tradition whose Talmud declares 'Better to be one of the persecuted than one of the persecutors' (Bava Kama) and 'A man should concern himself more that he not injure others than that he not be injured' (Tosfot to Baba Kama 23)'. Tamaret was born near Maltsh in 1869 and received a traditional orthodox education before spending two years in the Volozhin Yeshivah. He inherited the title of the Mileitchitzer Rav in 1893, where he worked for much of his life, excepting a period in Odessa. Unlike many orthodox rabbis of the time, he was not insular, and became a member of the Zionist movement. After attending the First Zionist conference, however, he became disillusioned, and turned against its nationalism. Also, hugely formative on Tamaret was the experience of the first world war, which convinced him that military violence was both futile and antithetical to genuine religion.

Much of Tamaret's work remains either unpublished or untranslated. While an anthology of his writings in Hebrew has been published (*Torah and Pacifism*, *Jerusalem*, The Dinur Center, 1992), the sole English translations are by Everett Gendler, both in a journal in the 1960s, and more recently in *Tikkun* magazine and at Arthur Waskow's Shalom Center. It is his translations that are quoted below.

In 'Passover and Non-Violence' Tamaret deals with the difficulty in separating attack and self defence:

HOW SHALL ONE DISCERN this faith which lies within the heart? Through deeds and actions which are appropriate to such a faith. This means that both individuals and entire peoples must order their lives on the basis of the saying recorded in the Tosefot to Baba Kama 23: "A man should concern himself more that he not injure others

than that he not be injured." For when a man tries to keep watch that his fist not injure others, by that very act he enthrones in the world the God of truth and righteousness and adds power to the kingdom of justice; and it is precisely this power which will defend him against injury by others.

This does not happen, however, if a man is preoccupied with watching out only for himself and keeps his fist always poised to prevent others attacking him; for by such a pose he in fact weakens the power of justice and stirs up evil. When a man constantly portrays to himself scenes of terror, when he asserts that everyone wants to obliterate him and that he can rely only on the power of his own fist, by this he denies the kingdom of truth and justice and enthrones the power of the fist. And since the fist is by nature poor at making distinctions, in the end defense and attack become reversed: instead of defending himself by means of the fist, such a man becomes himself the assailant and destroyer of others. Hence, like begetting like, others repay him in kind, and so the earth is filled with violence and oppression.

In 'The Congregation of Israel and the Wars of the Nations', Tamaret links nationalism to idolatry:

The dictum of the rabbis: 'Every house in which no words of torah are heard' (that is, any house not established upon the spirit of humility and the application of Torah, but rather upon the spirit of gross materialism) 'is bound to be destroyed' applies not only to a private house, but also to the abodes of whole peoples and nations. The Demon-Destroyer will not be content with the petty idols of the local taverns, of limited destructiveness, when from the base tendencies of men, he may carve a huge idol of such magnitude that its worship by all in the land will render his influence overwhelming and his strength sufficient to subdue all who kneel at its feet. The name of this monster-idol, fashioned by joining together all the private egotisms of individual citizens, is 'the honour of the fatherland'; its manner of worship – the slaughter of millions in wars for 'the native land'.

In 'Judaism and Freedom', Tamaret discusses the mission of Israel, and argues that it cannot be a purely spiritual one:

> Israel neither seeks nor will accept consolations or cures which are 'political' 'territorial' and so forth! We want none of these sorcerer's panaceas, medicines vain and worthless. Our sole healing is the purification of the spirit and the spreading of justice and compassion in the world. Indeed, the striving for justice and compassion is very near to us, upon our lips and in our hearts. It rests in our sacred scriptures, that glorious champion of justice and righteousness; and in crucible of the suffering of the exile, which has planted within us the feeling of compassion for the suffering of others . . . As for those who argue that the Jewish people has fulfilled its mission since all now admit 'the Oneness of the Creator', let them consider that 'not the teaching but the deed is primary'. What value is there in that the concept of God's unity has penetrated the minds of the nations if, sleek and satisfied, content and well fed, the divine illumination has failed to enter their hearts, which yet remain filled with oppression and haughtiness . . . It is for us, then to sit in our houses, trusting and confident, that ultimately our culture – the culture of 'the people of the Book' of a 'people driven and plucked' – will vanquish all the Edomite cultures: that cruelty will melt before compassion; that might will don garments of shame before the consecration of the kingdom of righteousness. Then happy and well shall it be for us, and happy and well for all the world'.

Elsewhere, Tamaret writes on the danger of Jews taking up arms:

> Small and humble is Jacob, and his ability to influence humanity for good is indeed limited. On the other hand, his ability to corrupt and pollute the moral atmosphere of the earth, should he pervert his way, is greater than anyone else's. For it unfortunately follows logically: if this frail and tender people, whose existence has always been secured by Moral Force, at last acknowledges the sword, how shall one answer those nations who have always lived by the Sword? . . .
>
> How terrible is that corruption which would result from any evil

example set by Jacob, selected by God, Israel, His special treasure
were he, also, at last to adopt the faith of Esau. . . . One may be sure
that when Jacob behaves deviously or dishonorably, the example will
be duly noted along with his distinction, and suddenly he will become
a valued authority who serves to sanction their own misdeeds. . . .

He also attacks mainstream Zionism in the strongest terms:

. . . Travellers to Israel never entered as simple immigrants, merely
desirous of a peaceful place in which to work and create a life for
themselves, a place which would satisfy their romantic desire to
hear echoes of the Biblical age still resounding on the mountains of
Judah and which would, in due course, nourish their spirits with that
revivifying air of the land of Israel. A modest arrival of this sort would
not have frightened and aroused the Arabs, and so it would have been
possible gradually to establish there, in the land of our ancestors, a
Hebrew settlement to the satisfaction of Jews everywhere, even though
this yishuv did not dream dreams of statehood and sovereignty, nor
presume to dominate Jews everywhere as teacher of all Jews in the
Diaspora. It would have been possible to establish a simple Jewish
settlement in the land of Israel like Jewish settlements everywhere
on this earth, that the land of our forefathers not be less than lands
elsewhere. Thus Jews in the land of Israel would have joined Jews
everywhere in waiting for the true coming of the Messiah, that ideal
moral redemption which is anticipated in Scripture and Rabbinic
Teachings. . . .

Armed with a piece of paper, the official obtained from Balfour, and
with that pride which comes from having seen the face of the king,
the Zionist leaders began to proclaim loudly and openly that they had
come to establish a Jewish State and to become lords of the land. They
further began to urge Jews to hasten from the four corners of the earth
to the land of Israel, not because Jews personally needed to emigrate,
but in order to achieve a Jewish majority and thereby become the
dominant people, outnumbering the original Arab inhabitants of the
land, who would then become a tolerated minority . . . the Zionists
hid their eyes from the fact that the actual place was not a newly

discovered, unsettled island located at the far ends of the earth but was a place already inhabited by a people which was sure to feel the nationalist and sovereign political aims as a needle in its living flesh.

. . . Thus the result resembles the tale told by Rabba bar bar Hanna (Baba Batra 73b). A group of seafarers saw a slope which from afar resembled an island, and so they approached, left their boats, and spent several days resting on it. During this interval they wandered about, spread themselves out, and soon felt like absolute owners of the place. Finally they lit a fire with which to bake bread and roast meat, and at last discovered that, although it had appeared to their eyes as a lump of inert clay, this was not an island but rather a living whale. As soon as the fire was felt by the fish, he turned on his back, quaked, raged, and tossed them all into the sea. Had their boats not been near to rescue them, they might have drowned in the sea. The application is painfully evident.

. . . For whoever builds a 'national refuge' acts mistakenly, conceding thereby the Sodomite measure by which the dwellers of this planet are declared to be either owners or intruders, with the former having the privilege of disposing of the latter as they see fit. Furthermore, such a one narrows the universal image of Judaism, demeans the image of Diaspora Jews, and casts upon them shadows of despair.

Tamaret's erudition, humanity and rhetorical skill are remarkable. His writings often sound like Gandhi, Tolstoy or like the radical English Christians, such as the Levellers, Diggers and Quakers, yet they are firmly based in Jewish tradition. Erich Fromm understands the importance of this point, noting that while

many outstanding Jews in the last one hundred and fifty years, like Marx, Einstein and others, who believed in and expressed the ideas of humanism but outside of the flow of Jewish tradition . . . Rabbi Tamaret's criticism of nationalism is written in the spirit of that tradition which has God forbid the angels to sing psalms of jubilation when the Egyptians were drowned – for the Egyptians were God's creatures.'

Of course, one figure does not make a movement. The writings of Tamaret alone will not overcome the hegemony of mainstream Jewish narratives, nor convert Jews overnight to a philosophy of non-violence. They can, however, start to sow seeds of doubt in the mind of all but the most conservative Jew that Judaism has more to say about war and peace than that said by Jabotinsky and Menachem Begin. They can show that pacifism and torah can sit side by side in an organic, natural fashion, without one being artificially grafted on to the other. They can, along with the writings of other figures, from Rosenzweig to Hannah Arendt to Derrida to Boyarin (no doubt also encompassing Aher and Korach) demonstrate that an alternative Jewish historiography is possible, embracing the outcasts, dreamers and humanists of Jewish history. Can there be a better tikkun than this?

Minutes from Jewdas meeting

Thanks for sending the Jewdas meeting minutes Karl,
Glad that Marie is doing so well in the BoD
Looks fab! Geoffrey

From: Karl M <karlyminst@blueyonder.co.uk>
To: All organisers list serv: <allorganiserslist@jewdas.com>

Sent: Tuesday, 28 August 2018, 1:03
Subject: Minutes from meeting 27/8/18

Hi all,

Sorry for being so late with getting the minutes out. Here are the notes and action points from the last meeting.

Remember that tomorrow is deadline for end of year dinner booking and award nominations!

Karl x

Jewdas meeting minutes
Monday 27th August 2018
Sternberg Centre

Attendees: Marie, Joseph, Annie, Jo, Joe, Simon, Yael T, Moshe, Yael L, Leah, Robin, Sue, Jon, Tim, Baruch, Yael W, Karl, Emma, Matt, Rachel, Deborah, Shira, Yael R, Sophia, Keith, Chaim

Apologies: Geoffrey, Elijah

Chair: Deborah
Minutes: Karl

1. **Updates from previous meeting**

   Minutes from previous meeting were approved

   ### Board of Deputies takeover

   Marie says it's going very well. Nobody believed that she was really Jewdas so she now says she's 'hiding in plain sight'. Mostly still settling in before she starts implementing Operation K, but has managed some subtle sabotage by pretending to be incompetent and sitting on emails

   ### Undermining Jewish Chronicle

   Sales are continuing to fall, but not fast enough. No new staff resignations since last update. Deborah and Yael T apologised, will work on getting more done. The rest of the group gave their thanks and affirmed that there was no need for apologies. Rachel needs to take a step back from writing Secret Shul Goer to focus on her family. Matt and Robin will plan a party to thank her for her work.

   ### Destroying the nuclear family

   Campaign to promote homosexuality and undermine the nuclear family is going well as normal. JW3 will do another LGBT week. Yael W is still working on turning Luciana Berger gay but no luck since their last date

   ### Website and social media

   Jo and Joe say the website is going well, especially since the redesign. Content has been lower because of both being away on August holidays in Cuba but followers have still gone up by 1,000 on Facebook and 257 on Twitter. Plans to leak details of Israeli nuclear programme have been delayed, to be reviewed at next meeting when Geoffrey is here.

2. **Budget**

   Incoming: Beetroot was eventually sold to Rausing for £5,000. Although not as much as hoped, it will partly fund our holiday to Amsterdam

   Soros has sent us £10,000 for activism costs, provided it isn't spent on staffing. Annie will chase up Ahmadinejad to see if he can cover additional staffing expenses

Simon suggested we give up fundraising for a spy dolphin. A brief vote was taken, and we have agreed to keep trying to get enough money for the dolphin by 24 votes to 1 with 1 abstention (Deborah as she was chairing)

3. **Antisemitism screening service**

The launch of the Jewdas ASS was successful, due to excellent promotion by our social media department. To date the ASS has responded to 315 enquiries. Total income was £1,314, and staff costs were £800, providing a modest profit of £514 which will be reinvested back into the service.

Service	Number of enquiries	Income
Simple yes/no/maybe answer £3	268	£804
Extended response £10	45	£450
Experienced stylist £30	2	£60
Total	**315**	**£1314**

Answered yes to all the £3 questions to save time. Need to give a detailed analysis on why Ken Livingstone was antisemitic. 40 out of 45 questions were about it. Yael L will write up by end of August.

4. **Comrade B**

The working group has met with comrade B following them repeatedly mispronouncing beigel. Comrade B has completed the necessary political reeducation classes and will be welcomed back to our gatherings. Please be vigilant for any bagel-sayers in our midst.

5. **Jewdas Goy of the Year awards**

The end of year dinner and awards committee reported that preparations are going well. They reminded comrades to send their nominations to Sophia ASAP before the deadline next Thursday. Awards will be announced at the end of year dinner.

6. **Campaign for better kiddushes**

Simon and Shira presented their campaign proposal, and the idea was approved. They will start the first phase of the campaign which

maybe

is to research the kiddushes available at various shuls to assess which communities most need our help. If you would like to join the campaign team then please contact Simon or Shira directly.

7. Revolution

Please note that the date for the revolution has been pushed back again to 14th November as Robin has a dentist appointment on the original date.

8. Promoting diasporism in Masorti

As we discussed at the last meeting, we are using the name 'Ohel Mo'ed' as a front for promoting diasporism in Masorti. Thank you to the comrades who have been taking part, spending large amounts of time pretending to be interested in halacha in order to distract the masorti movement from participating in hasbara. Anybody who doesn't mind mumbling and lives in north west London should contact Chaim for further info.

9. International updates

Spanish comrades have now fully taken over the Chabad House in Ibiza. This follows on from successful seizures of the ones in Izmir and Helsinki last year. We are hoping to take the one in Buenos Aires next year.

Max got in touch to say that Assad would be happy to pay for us to come to Syria on a BirthWrong tour. Certain ideological objections were raised and we agreed to politely decline. Yael W will write to him.

10. AOB

Karl has raised the issue that we are out of lox. He will buy some on the way home.

Keith has again asked everyone to read their emails in advance so that our meetings can be shorter

Next meeting: Sunday 30th September

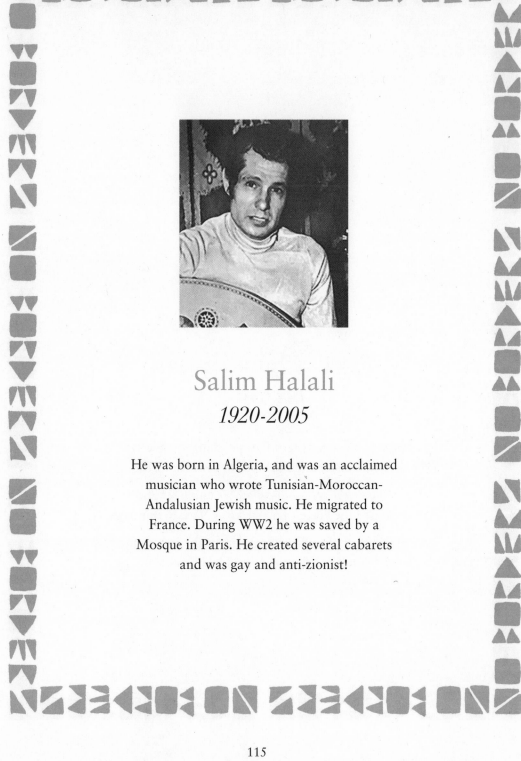

Salim Halali
1920-2005

He was born in Algeria, and was an acclaimed
musician who wrote Tunisian-Moroccan-
Andalusian Jewish music. He migrated to
France. During WW2 he was saved by a
Mosque in Paris. He created several cabarets
and was gay and anti-zionist!

Rose Schneiderman
1882-1972

She was born in eastern Europe, came to New York
as a child and started to work in garment factories.

She was a grassroots women's unioniser and
organised the biggest rent strike in NYC to this day.

Her speech after the triangle shirtwaist factory fire
inspired the song bread and roses.

She was gay!

Milly Witkop
1877-1955

She was a prominent London Jewish east end anarchist. She is amazing, and Rudolf Rocker gets all the credit for her work.

She co-edited the Jewish anarchist London newspaper, Arbeyter Fraynd.

Avraam Benroya

1887-1979

He was born in Bulgaria and then moved to Salonika,
the diaspora city that had a Jewish majority.

Like a true Jewish lefty he founded about 70 million
different organisations which were essentially the same
but with slightly different names. He also founded a
ladino socialist newsletter.

His vision was of a state without religious or ethnic
divisions, where many different people can live together
in peace and without discrimination. He believed that
this could only be achieved through workers unity.

Having survived the Mussolini regime and Nazi
concentration camps, he died in poverty in Israel.

 Glossary

Beigel:	The greatest controversy facing the Jewish community today. Strictly religious Jews can be found davening with their noses pressed up against the windows of Beigel Bake in Shoreditch. During Pesach, we let beigels be bygones as nobody is allowed to eat them anyway.
Board of Deputies	This was previously the official voice of the Jewish community. In April 2018, we surpassed them in Twitter followers and received a letter from The Queen informing us that we were now the sole representatives. The Board of Deputies has repeatedly applied to join Jewdas, but has been rejected because we are not convinced they are really Jews.
Broiges:	A type of fun.
Chametz:	Carbs.
Diaspora:	Where you live. Except you. You know who you are. Not you.
Elijah:	Bringer of revolution.
FPR:	(Food to Propaganda Ratio): A system of assessing the worthiness of any event. The numerator consists of scores for quality and quantity of food. The denominator takes into account the content and boringness of any propaganda. 10 = all food, no propaganda. 5 = no food, all propaganda.
Geoffrey Cohen:	In every generation, every baby has the potential to become Geoffrey Cohen. In the biblical period, Geoffrey was Korach. In the time of the rabbis, it was Anan ben David. In the late medieval period, it was Shabbetai Zvi. Today, Geoffrey is a 44-year-old lesbian mother-of-3 who lives in a bedsit in Slough. She is the sole author of this haggadah and all core heretical Jewish writings.

God:	Mythical creature. Famous examples of God include the pointing index finger on the Sistine Chapel ceiling, and Beyoncé.
Goy:	Like a Jew, but less so.
Haggadah:	What you're reading. Not usually this fun, with the exception of the children's version with the pull-out slides.
Israel:	Israel can refer to the Biblical figure Jacob, the Jewish people, the Jewish religious community, a historic land between the Nile and the Euphrates, a future promised place, probably in space, where we will finally achieve fully automated luxury gay space communism, or the modern racist apartheid state. Choose your own adventure. If you've chosen adventure number 7, this might not be the haggadah for you.
Jew:	Like a goy, but more so.
Jewish Chronicle	Describes itself as the organ of British Jewry. We all know which organ.
Jewish:	Not a language.
Judaism:	4000-year-old cult involving strange laws, lavish rituals, good food and explaining Israel to goyim. Also, we invented fish and chips. Famous Jews include Amy Winehouse, Craig David and Ed Miliband (but not David).
Kiddush:	The blessing said over wine on Shabbes, or, the highlight of shul.
Kosher:	Blessed food that's double the price.
London:	A metropolitan city to the south of Sheffield.
Matzah:	Think cream crackers, but without the cream. Or the flavour. Like big communion wafers. Like really bad roti.
Mitzrayim:	The place you leave to find liberation. See 'capitalism'.
Rabbi:	Man with black hat, beard and Eastern Ashkenazi accent. Famous rabbis include Julia Neuberger, Laura

Janner-Klausner, Azenath Barazani and Regina Jonas.

Responsum: Occasionally, rabbis send round answers to questions nobody asked.

Satire: Like lying, but funny.

Sheffield: The eternal capital of the Jewish people.

Shoreditch: A wanky bit of London that used to have a lot of Jews living there.

Talmud: The longest facebook post.

Torah: A book. Every time you refer to this as the 'Old Testament', a puppy loses its wings.

Zionist: Somebody who believes that there should be a Jewish state in the historic land of Palestine. Not necessarily a racist, but probably.

The End of the Hagaddah

You have either finished your seder or opened the book the wrong way round like a schmuck. If it's the former, mazal tov! Go and sleep off all that wine and matzo. If it's the latter, you probably want to turn the book over and try again.

Unlike most scripts, the Hebrew alphabet is written right-to-left. The predominant theory for why that is, before the invention of parchment and ink, scholars would engrave written language into stone. When you're busy chiselling you're not so worried about smudging. Scribes would hold a hammer in their stronger right hand and their chisel (or sickle, depending on their activity) in their left.

Of course there are a load of nonsense reasons for why we as Jews might prefer to go from right to left, but Rav Geoffrey Cohen explained that we write in this direction to remind ourselves of the inevitable and relentless march of history from oppression to liberation.